10

MINUTE GUIDE TO

WORD FOR WINDOWS 95

by Peter Aitken

A Division of Macmillan Computer Publishing
201 West 103rd St., Indianapolis, Indiana 46290 USA

International Standard Book Number: 0-7897-0379-3
Library of Congress Catalog Card Number: 94-73408

98   8 7 6

Interpretation of the printing code: the rightmost number of the first series of numbers is the year of the book's printing; the rightmost number of the second series of numbers is the number of the book's printing. For example, a printing code of 95-1 shows that the first printing of the book occurred in 1995.

Screen reproductions in this book were created by means of the program Collage Plus from Inner Media, Inc., Hollis, NH.

Printed in the United States of America

Publisher Roland Elgey

Vice-President and Publisher Marie Butler-Knight

Editorial Services Director Elizabeth Keaffaber

Publishing Manager Barry Pruett

Managing Editor Michael Cunningham

Development Editor David Bradford

Technical Editor Herb Feltner

Production Editor Phil Kitchel

Copy Editor Silvette Pope

Cover Designer Scott Cook

Designer Barbara Kordesh

Production Analysts Angela Bannan & Bobbi Satterfield

Indexer Debra Myers

Production Team Maxine Dillingham, Joan Evan, DiMonique Ford, John Hulse, Damon Jordan, Barry Jorden, Kaylene Riemen, Scott Tullis, Kelly Warner, Jody York

CONTENTS

Introduction

Welcome to Microsoft Word for Windows 95. Coinciding with the release of the long-awaited Windows 95 operating system, the new Word, Version 7, continues to build upon its reputation as a powerful and flexible word processing program. Word provides everything you need to create anything from a one-page memo to a polished, 500-page report. No wonder it has become the word processor of choice for millions of people.

Word's designers put a lot of effort into making the program easy to use. Still, any program with so much power is, unavoidably, somewhat complex. Given Word's hundreds of features, you may find yourself lost looking for the one thing you need. Sure, you could buy one of those 800-page books on Word you've seen at the bookstore, but do you have time to read it? Probably not—what you need is a fast method of learning the program's most important features, those features that people use most often in their day-to-day word processing tasks.

I'm glad to say that you bought the right book! *The 10 Minute Guide to Word for Windows 95* is just what you're looking for. This book presents you with the basics of Word in a series of short, easy-to-digest lessons. Each lesson is self-contained and can be completed in 10 minutes or less, allowing you to start and stop as your schedule allows.

What Is the Ten Minute Guide?

The *10 Minute Guide* series takes a different approach to teaching you how to use a computer program. We make no effort to cover every detail of a program. Rather, the *Guide* concentrates on those features that are essential for most users - those features that you need to get your work done! The goal is to get you to where you can start using the program for productive work, as quickly as possible.

Conventions Used in this Book

Throughout the book, the following icons are used to help you find information more quickly:

 Plain English   New or unfamiliar terms are explained for you in straightforward, everyday language.

 Timesaver Tip   These tips offer hints and shortcuts to help you use the program efficiently.

 Panic Button   This icon warns you of potential problems and offers practical solutions.

In addition, the following conventions are used to organize the book's material:

- Numbered steps provide exact instructions for frequently needed procedures.

- Text that you enter and commands and options that you select are printed in bold color.

- Menu commands, dialog box selections, and commands are printed with the first letter capitalized for easy recognition.

- Messages that appear on-screen are displayed in a special, monospaced font.

Using This Book

On the inside front cover of the book you'll find concise instructions for installing Word for Windows on your system. The inside back cover features a guide to the on-line Help system.

This book contains 31 lessons. I suggest that you work through them in order. After reading the first seven lessons, however, you can jump around to find specific information quickly. Once you have read all the lessons you will have a good grounding in the most important features of the Word for Windows program. If you want to go further and explore the program's many advanced features, I recommend Special Edition Using Word for Windows 95.

If You're Upgrading

Readers who are familiar with Word 6 are probably interested in finding out about Version 7's new features. You should turn first to Appendix A, which briefly describes the new features and refers you to the lesson where each new feature is covered.

Trademarks

All terms mentioned in this book that are known to be trademarks or service marks are listed below. In addition, terms that are suspected of being trademarks or service marks have been capitalized. Que Corporation cannot attest to the accuracy of this information. Use of a term in this book should not be regarded as affecting the validity of any trademark or service mark.

AutoCAD is a registered trademark of Autodesk Inc.

Micrografx is a registered trademark of Micrografx Inc.

Windows and Toolbar are trademarks of Microsoft Corporation.

GETTING STARTED

In this lesson, you'll start Microsoft Word for Windows 95, learn the parts of the Word for Windows screen, and learn how to quit the program. You'll also learn about the toolbar.

STARTING WORD FOR WINDOWS

To start Word for Windows, you must first install it on your system. See the inside front cover of this book for default installation instructions. After you install Word for Windows, your Windows desktop screen will include a Winword window, and that window will contain a Microsoft Word icon. If you are using Microsoft Office, the Winword icon will be located in the Microsoft Office window. To start the program, double-click the icon. You can also start Word by selecting it from the Programs section of the Windows Start menu.

What's an Icon? An *icon* is a small graphic symbol that Windows uses to represent a program or screen window.

The Waiting Game While the mouse pointer is an hourglass, you must wait.

PARTS OF THE SCREEN

When you start Word for Windows, you will see its opening logo for a few seconds and then the main screen appears with a blank document, ready for your input. Take a moment to familiarize yourself with the Word for Windows screen. It contains a number of useful components, as shown in Figure 1.1.

Title bar   Displays the program name and the name of the document being edited.

Menu bar   Contains the main Word for Windows menu.

Standard toolbar   Displays buttons that you can select to perform common editing tasks. You must have a mouse to use the toolbar.

Formatting toolbar   Use to select character- and paragraph-formatting commands. You must have a mouse to use this toolbar, too.

TipWizard   Displays helpful tips about using Word. This is a new feature in Word for Windows 95.

Ruler   Controls margins, indents, and tab stops.

Work area   Where your document appears.

Scroll bars   Use to move around your document with the mouse.

Status bar   Displays information about your document.

Windows Taskbar   Part of Windows 95. Displays the time and can be used to switch between programs.

Standard toolbar   Title bar   Menu bar   TipWizard

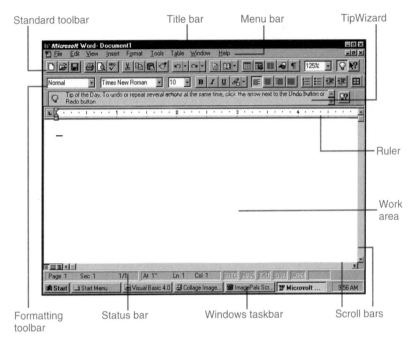

Ruler

Work area

Formatting toolbar   Status bar   Windows taskbar   Scroll bars

FIGURE 1.1   Components of the Word for Windows screen.

Depending on how you set up your system, one or more of these screen components may not appear. Don't worry—you'll see how to display them later.

THE TOOLBAR

The toolbar contains buttons that you select with the mouse to perform common tasks. For example, the far left button on the Standard toolbar represents the File New command, and the button next to it represents the File Open command. If you position the mouse pointer on
a toolbar button (without clicking) Word displays a *tool tip* next to the mouse pointer, with a brief description of the button's

function.

You'll probably find that clicking a toolbar button is quicker and more convenient than entering the entire command sequence.

QUITTING WORD FOR WINDOWS

When you finish using Word for Windows, quit the program by doing one of the following:

- Press Alt+F4 on the keyboard.

- With the mouse, position the pointer on the box at the left of the title bar and double-click.

- Click the Close button (the button with the **X**) at the right of the title bar.

- Select the Exit command from the File menu on the Menu bar.

If you have any unsaved documents, Word for Windows prompts you to save them. Then the program terminates, and you return to the Windows desktop.

In this lesson, you learned how to start and quit Word for Windows and about the parts of the screen. In the next lesson, you'll learn how to use the Word for Windows Help system.

THE HELP SYSTEM

In this lesson, you'll learn how to use Word's online Help system.

THE HELP COMMAND

The Help command lets you access Word's online Help system, which can display program information and instructions on your screen. One way to access the Help system is via the Help command on the main menu. This menu has five commands on it:

- **Microsoft Word Help Topics** displays the main Help screen, titled Help Topics.

- **Answer Wizard** starts the Word Answer Wizard (which you can also access via the Help Topics screen).

- **The Microsoft Network** lets you connect to the Microsoft Network. This command is available only if you've set up your system for the network connection.

- **WordPerfect Help** displays help for users who are familiar with the WordPerfect word processing program.

- **About Microsoft Word** displays information about the Word for Windows program, such as the program version number and the license number.

This lesson explains the most useful parts of the Help system in this lesson. Please refer to your program documentation if you want additional information on the Microsoft Network or WordPerfect Help.

Quick Help   You can display the Help Topics screen as you edit your document by pressing F1 .

THE HELP TOPICS SCREEN

The Help Topics screen has four tabs that let you access different parts of the Help system.

CONTENTS

See the **Contents** tab in Figure 2.1. Each title, or *book*, in the list describes a section of the Help material. To open a book, select it, and then click the Open button. To close an open book, double-click the open-book icon next to the title.

FIGURE 2.1   The Contents tab on the Help Topics screen.

When you open a book, a list of its chapters appear, as shown in Figure 2.2. A question-mark icon marks the book chapters. To open a chapter, click the question-mark icon, and then click Open . A book may also contain other books, which you can open the same way.

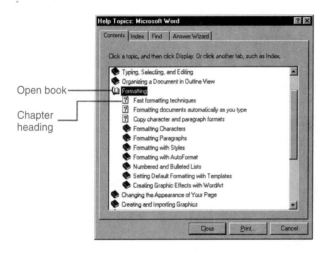

Open book

Chapter heading

FIGURE 2.2 An opened Help book displays its chapter headings.

Two different Help screens may appear when you open a chapter. One is a graphical screen that provides a picture of the selected topic. This type of screen (see Figure 2.3) has labels that you can click to display additional information on a specific task or topic.

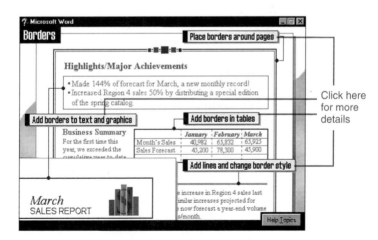

Click here for more details

FIGURE 2.3 A graphical Help screen.

A text screen also provides Help information, as shown in Figure 2.4. Many text screens have buttons you can click for more information.

Click these buttons for more information

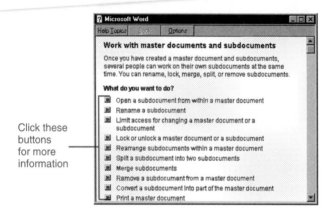

FIGURE 2.4   A text Help screen.

On any Help screen, click the Help Topics button to close the Help screen and return to the Help Topics window. Or press Esc to close the Help screen and return to your document.

INDEX

The **Index** tab provides an alphabetical list of Help topics, as shown in Figure 2.5. You can scroll through the list to find the one of interest, or you can start typing a word in the first box; the list will automatically scroll to the proper section. Click the topic you want in the list, and then click the Display button. If you want to scroll through the list, you can click the scroll bar arrows to search for a topic.

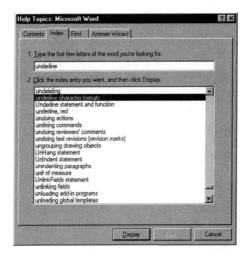

FIGURE 2.5 The Index tab on the Help Topics screen.

FIND

The Find tab in the Help Topics window (Figure 2.6) lets you search the Help system for the topic you need.

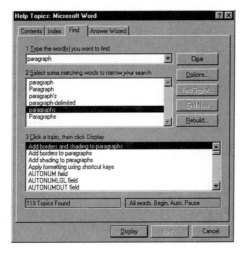

FIGURE 2.6 The Find tab on the Help Topics screen.

To use the Find tab:

1. Type the term or topic you want to find in the first box.

2. In the second box, click the term or topic that most closely matches the term you typed.

3. The third box displays a list of Help topics that related to the selected term. Click the desired topic and then click the Display button.

Word displays a Help screen with information on the selected topic.

ANSWER WIZARD

The Answer Wizard lets you find Help information by asking questions in your own words. It's one of Word 7.0's new features. You can access the *Answer Wizard* by selecting Answer Wizard from the Help menu, or by selecting the Answer Wizard tab in the **Help Topics** screen. The Answer Wizard provides an unusual way for you to obtain Help information, as shown in Figure 2.7.

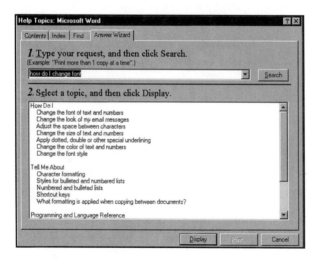

FIGURE 2.7   The Answer Wizard.

To use the Answer Wizard, type a question or request into the **number 1** text box on the Answer Wizard screen, and then press Enter or click the Search button. You may be wondering how you check spelling. Word displays a list of topics that it thinks might answer your question. Click the topic you want to view, and then click the Display button. For most topics, Word then displays a Help screen with the relevant information. In some cases, Word will "demonstrate" the task to you by issuing the needed menu commands.

THE TIP WIZARD

When the Tip Wizard is active, it "watches" you work and displays helpful hints about what you are doing. The Tip Wizard appears below the Formatting toolbar, as shown in Figure 2.8. In this figure, the Tip Wizard displays a tip about Word's automatic spell-checking feature (which you'll learn about in Lesson 21).

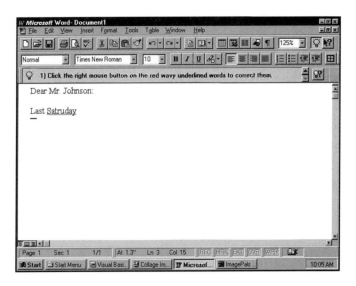

FIGURE 2.8   The Tip Wizard displays helpful hints about what you are doing.

To turn the Tip Wizard display on or off, select View Toolbars, and then click the Tip Wizard option. When the Tip Wizard is turned on, it detects you doing certain things and flashes the yellow light bulb in its window; you will see a tip or hint. You can scroll through previously displayed tips using the scroll bar at the right end of the Tip Wizard window.

Normally, the Tip Wizard displays each tip only once. To reset the Tip Wizard so that it will display previous tips again in the future, press Ctrl and click the light bulb on the Tip Wizard.

If the Tip Wizard appears but does not display any tips, you may need to activate it:

1. Select Tools Options to display the Options dialog box.

2. Click the General tab, if necessary.

3. Click the TipWizard Active option to turn it on.

4. Select OK.

Context-Sensitive Help

If you are using Word's menus or dialog boxes, you can obtain context-sensitive Help at any time by pressing F1. If you highlight a menu command, information about that command appears. If you see a dialog box is open, pressing F1 displays information about the dialog box.

After you have read Help, press Esc to close it and return to what you were doing.

 Context-sensitive Help   Information directly related to what you are doing at the moment.

In this lesson, you learned how to use the Help system. In the next lesson, you'll learn how to enter and delete text, and how to move around a document.

CREATING A NEW DOCUMENT

In this lesson, you'll learn how to enter text, how to move around the screen, and how to select and delete text.

ENTERING TEXT

When starting Word for Windows 95, you see a blank work area that contains only two items:

- **Blinking vertical line**   Marks the insertion point, the location where text you type appears in the document and where certain editing actions occurs.

- **Horizontal line**   The end-of-document marker.

Since your new document is empty, these two markers are at the same location. To enter text, simply type it by using the keyboard. As you type, the text appears and the insertion point moves to the right. If the line reaches the right edge of the screen, then Word automatically moves to the start of the next line; this is *word wrapping*. Press Enter only when you want to start a new paragraph. As you enter more lines than will fit on the screen, Word for Windows 95 automatically scrolls previously entered text upward to keep the insertion point in view.

Leave It to Word Wrap   Press Enter only when you want to start a new paragraph.

MOVING AROUND THE SCREEN

As you work on a document, you will often have to move the insertion point so that you can view or work on other regions of text.

TABLE 3.1   MOVING THE INSERTION POINT AROUND THE SCREEN

TO MOVE	PERFORM THIS ACTION
With the mouse	
Up or down one line	Click the up or down arrow on the vertical scroll bar.
Up or down one screen	Click the vertical scroll bar between the box and the up or down arrow.
Up or down any amount	Drag the scroll bar box up or down.
To any visible location	Click the location.
With the keyboard	
Left or right one character	Press ← or →.
Up or down one line	Press ↑ or ↓.
Left or right one word	Press Ctrl+ ← or Ctrl+→.
Up or down one paragraph	Press Ctrl+↑ or Ctrl+↓.
Start or end of a line	Press Home or End.
Up or down one screen	Press PgUp or PgDn.
Top or bottom of current screen	Press Ctrl+PgUp or Ctrl+PgDn.
Start or end of the document	Press Ctrl+Home or Ctrl+End.

SELECTING TEXT

Many Word for Windows 95 operations require that you first *select* the text that you want to modify. For example, to italicize a word, you must select the word first and then specify italics. Selected text appears on the screen in reverse video, as shown in Figure 3.1, which has the phrase **Dear Mr. Johnson** selected.

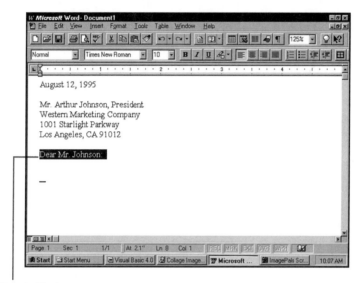

Selected text

FIGURE 3.1   Selected text appears in reverse video.

You can select text with either the mouse or the keyboard. With the mouse, you can use the *selection bar*, an unmarked column in the left document margin. When the mouse pointer moves from the document to the selection bar, it changes from an I-beam to an arrow.

TABLE 3.2   METHODS OF SELECTING TEXT

TO SELECT TEXT	PERFORM THIS ACTION
With the mouse	
Any amount	Point at the start of the text; drag the highlight over the text.
One word	Double-click anywhere on the word.
One sentence	Press and hold Ctrl and click anywhere in the sentence.
One line	Click the selection bar next to the line.
Multiple lines	Drag in the selection bar next to the lines.
One paragraph	Double-click the selection bar next to the paragraph.
Entire document	Press and hold Ctrl and click anywhere in the selection bar.
With the keyboard	
Any amount	Move the insertion point to the start of the text, press and hold Shift, and move the insertion point to the end of the desired text using the movement keys described earlier.
Entire document	Ctrl+A.

To cancel a selection, click anywhere on the screen or use the keyboard to move the insertion point.

TIP   **Fast Select**   Double-click a word to select it quickly.

DELETING TEXT

You can delete single characters or larger blocks of text.

- To delete the character to the right of the insertion point, press Del.

- To delete the character to the left of the insertion point, press Backspace.

- To delete a block of text, select the text and then press Del or Backspace.

If you make a mistake, you can recover deleted text with the **Edit Undo** command. Depending on how you deleted the text, this command appears on the Edit menu as either Undo Typing or Undo Edit Clear. In either case, the effect is the same: the deleted characters are replaced in their original position. You must select this command immediately after deleting and before performing any other action. You can also click on the Undo button on the Toolbar or press the shortcut key, **Ctrl+Z**. You can select Undo more than once to undo several most recent editing actions.

In this lesson, you learned how to enter, select, and delete text. In the next lesson, you'll learn how to create a new document using Word's templates and Wizards.

4 LESSON

USING TEMPLATES AND WIZARDS

In this lesson, you'll learn how to use Word's templates and wizards to create a new document.

DOCUMENTS AND TEMPLATES

As you learned in the previous lesson, when you start Word, it displays a blank document for you to work with. The new document uses Word's Normal template. The question is, what is a template?

You may not be aware of it, but every Word for Windows document uses a *template*. A template is a model, or pattern, for a document. A template can contain boilerplate text, graphics, and formatting. It can also contain styles, glossary entries, and macros (covered in later lessons). Any document that uses a template automatically contains all the elements of the template. Then, you add additional text and formatting as needed.

For example, a business-letter template might contain your company's logo and address, the date, and a salutation. When you use the template, you need to type in only the text of the letter; the standard elements are provided by the template. You can create your own templates (as you'll learn in a later lesson); you can also use the predefined templates that come with Word.

SPECIALIZED TEMPLATES

The Normal template is pretty basic; it contains no boilerplate text or special formatting. It is fine for many documents. However, Word provides a variety of specialized templates that are designed to simplify the task of creating certain types of documents, such as FAXes, memos, invoices, newsletters, and more.

 Roll Your Own You'll learn how to create your own templates in Lesson 16.

WIZARDS

A wizard goes a step beyond a regular template. In addition to providing predefined formatting and text, a wizard automates part of the process of creating a document. For example, a FAX Wizard would prompt you to enter the recipient's name and telephone number, and then automatically insert them in the proper locations in the document.

CREATING A NEW DOCUMENT FROM A TEMPLATE

Here are the steps for creating a new document based on a template:

1. Select File New. Word displays the New dialog box, shown in Figure 4.1.

2. Click the tab corresponding to the type of document you are creating. The figure shows the Letters & Faxes tab selected.

3. Click the desired template.

4. Select OK.

Template icon —
Wizard icon —

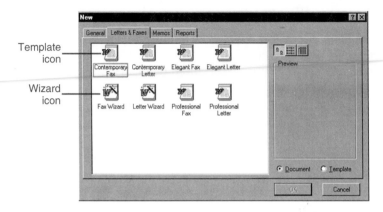

Figure 4.1   The New dialog box lists available templates.

Click Yourself a New Document   To create a new document based on the Normal template, click the New button on the Standard toolbar.

Word will load the template. If the template contains any text, it will appear on your screen. You can now edit the document in the usual fashion. If you selected a wizard in step 3, see the next section for details on how to use it.

Using a Wizard

Each Word wizard is different, so it's impossible to provide detailed instructions that will apply to all of them. However, the basic steps involved are similar for all wizards. Once you understand these steps, you can handle any of the Word for Windows wizards.

A Wizard consists of a series of dialog boxes. Each dialog box presents you with options to select or text boxes where you enter information. A typical wizard dialog box is shown in Figure 4.2.

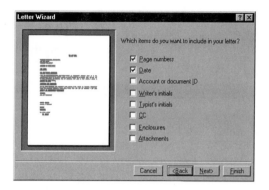

Figure 4.2   A typical wizard dialog box.

A simple wizard might have only two or three dialog boxes; a more complex one may have a dozen. After entering the required information in a dialog box, here's what to do:

- Click the Next button to go on to the next wizard dialog box. In the last dialog box, the Next button is not available.

- If you want to change information that you entered, click the Back button to return to the previous dialog box.

- If you want the Wizard to create the document using the information you have entered so far, click the Finish button.

- Click the Cancel button to cancel the wizard (your document will not be created).

Once the Wizard finishes, you can edit your new document using the standard techniques.

In this lesson, you learned how to use Word's templates and wizards to simplify the task of creating a new document. In the next lesson, you'll learn how to control the way Word displays documents on your screen.

5

CONTROLLING THE SCREEN DISPLAY

In this lesson, you'll learn how to control the Word for Windows screen display to suit your working style.

DOCUMENT DISPLAY MODES

Word for Windows offers four different views in which you can display your document.

NORMAL MODE

You'll probably want to work most often in *Normal* mode. This is the Word for Windows default display. Figure 5.1 shows a document in Normal view. As you can see, all special formatting is visible on-screen. Different font sizes, italics, boldface, and other enhancements display on the screen very much as they will appear on the printed page. Certain aspects of the page layout, however, are not displayed in order to speed editing; for example, you do not see headers and footers. Normal mode is fine for most editing tasks.

To select or change your view to Normal, select View Normal or click the Normal View button at the left end of the horizontal scroll bar. In the View menu, the currently selected mode has a dot displayed next to it.

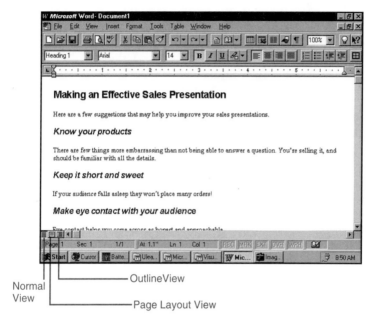

Normal View

OutlineView

Page Layout View

FIGURE 5.1 A document displayed in Normal mode.

OUTLINE MODE

Use *Outline* mode to create outlines and to examine the structure of a document. Figure 5.2 shows the sample document in Outline mode. Here you can choose to view only your document headings—hiding all subordinate text. You can quickly promote, demote, or move document headings—along with subordinate text—to a new location. For this to be useful, you need to assign heading styles to the document headings, a technique you'll learn more about in Lesson 24.

Select View Outline to switch to Outline view, or click the Outline View button at the left end of the horizontal scroll bar.

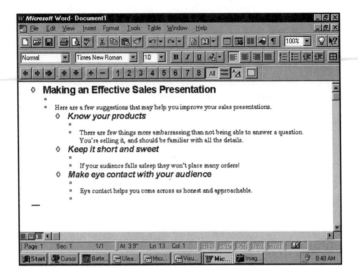

FIGURE 5.2   A document displayed in Outline mode.

PAGE LAYOUT MODE

Page Layout mode displays your document exactly as it will print. Headers, footers, and all the details of page layout appear on the screen. You can edit in Page Layout mode; this mode is ideal when you are fine-tuning the details of page composition. Be aware, however, that the additional computer processing required makes display changes relatively slow in Page Layout mode, particularly when you have a complex page layout. Figure 5.3 shows the sample document in Page Layout mode.

TIP   **Sneak Preview**   Use Page Layout mode to see what your printed document will look like before you actually print.

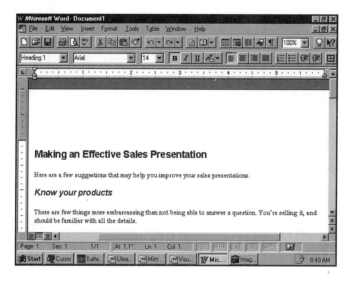

FIGURE 5.3 A document displayed in Page Layout mode.

Select View Page Layout, or click the Page Layout View button, to switch to Page Layout view.

DRAFT FONT MODE

Draft Font mode is a display option that you can apply in both Normal and Outline views. As Figure 5.4 illustrates, a single generic font appears on-screen and special formatting such as italics and boldface are indicated by underlining. Draft Font mode provides the fastest editing and screen display. This component is ideal when you're concentrating on the contents of your document rather than its appearance.

To turn Draft Font mode on or off:

1. Select Tools Options to display the Options dialog box.

2. If necessary, click the View tab to display the View options.

3. Select the Draft Font option to turn it on or off.

4. Select OK.

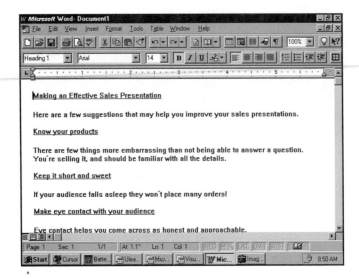

FIGURE 5.4   A document displayed in Draft mode.

FULL SCREEN DISPLAY

To see the maximum amount of text on the screen, select View Full Screen. In Full Screen mode, the title bar, menu, toolbars, status line, and all other Word elements are hidden, and you can use the full screen for your text. You can enter and edit text in this mode and select from the menus using the usual keyboard commands. To turn off Full Screen mode, select View Full Screen again, or click the Full Screen icon that appears in the lower right corner of the screen.

RULER AND TOOLBAR DISPLAY

The Word for Windows default is to display the ruler, Standard toolbar, and Formatting toolbar at the top of the editing screen. The TipWizard usually appears, too. At times, you may want to hide one or more of these items to give yourself a larger work area and a less-cluttered screen. Of course, you will not have access to the editing features of the item(s) you have hidden.

To control the screen display of the ruler, select View to display the View menu, and then select Ruler to toggle the ruler display between on and off. To control the toolbars and the TipWizard, select View Toolbars to display the Toolbars dialog box. Turn the Standard, Formatting, and TipWizard options on or off as desired, then select OK.

 Put 'em Away   Hide the ruler and toolbars when you need maximum text displayed but don't want to use Full Screen mode.

ZOOMING THE SCREEN

The View Zoom command lets you control the size of your document as displayed on the screen. You can enlarge it to facilitate reading small fonts or decrease the size to view an entire page at one time. When you select View Zoom, the Zoom dialog box appears (see Figure 5.5).

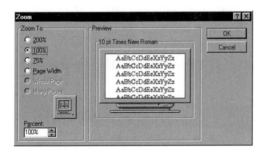

FIGURE 5.5   The Zoom dialog box.

In the Zoom dialog box, you have the following options. As you make selections, the Preview section of the dialog box shows you what the selected zoom setting will look like.

- Under **Zoom To**, select the desired page magnification. 200 percent is twice normal size, 75 percent is three-quarters normal size, and so on. In the **Percent** box, you can enter a custom magnification in the range 10–200 percent.

- Select Page Width to have Word for Windows automatically scale the display to fit the entire page width on the screen.

- Select Whole Page to have Word for Windows automatically scale the display to fit the entire page on the screen.

- Select Many Pages to display two or more pages at the same time. Click the monitor button under the **Many Pages** option, and then drag to specify how many pages to display.

- You can also change the zoom setting by pulling down the Zoom control on the Standard toolbar and selecting the desired zoom setting. This control is shown in Figure 5.4.

Note that the **Whole Page** and **Many Pages** options are available only if you are viewing the document in Page Layout mode.

In this lesson, you learned how to control the Word for Windows screen display. In the next lesson, you'll learn how to save documents.

SAVING DOCUMENTS

In this lesson, you'll learn how to name your document, save it to disk, and enter summary information.

SAVING A DOCUMENT FOR THE FIRST TIME

When you create a new document in Word for Windows, it is stored temporarily in your computer's memory under the default name Doc*n*, where *n* is a number that increases by 1 for each new unnamed document. The document is only "remembered" until you quit the program or the computer is turned off. To save a document permanently so you can retrieve it later, you must save it to a disk. This is done with the File Save command, or by selecting the Save button on the toolbar.

1. When you save a document for the first time, you must assign it another name. When you select File Save for an unnamed document (or File Save As for any document), Word displays the Save As dialog box, as shown in Figure 6.1.

2. In the **File name** text box, enter the name you want to assign to the document file. The name can be up to 256 characters long. If you want to save the document in a different folder, pull down the **Save in** list to select a different folder. Then select Save. Word for Windows automatically adds the DOC extension when it saves the file.

Save in list

File name box

FIGURE 6.1   The Save As dialog box.

What's an Extension?   The extension is the one- to three-letter part of a file name to the right of the period.

Next, Word for Windows displays the Properties dialog box, (see Figure 6.2). This figure (with the Summary tab selected) shows typical summary information that you might want to use. You can either ignore this dialog box or enter information here that will later be useful in keeping track of your documents.

- **Title**   Enter the title of the document. This is not the same as the document's file name.

- **Subject**   Enter a phrase describing the subject of the document.

- **Author**   Word automatically fills this field with the user name you entered when installing the program. You can change it if you like.

- **Keywords**   Enter one or more words related to the document contents.

- **Comments**   Enter any information you want saved with the document.

- **Statistics**   Click the Statistics tab to display information about the document, such as number of words, last date edited, and so on.

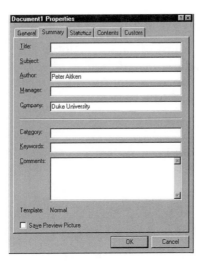

FIGURE 6.2   The Properties dialog box.

Summary Info Box Doesn't Display?   Select Properties
from the File menu to display it. Select Options from the
Tools menu, click the Save tab, and click the Prompt for
Document Properties option to control automatic display
of the Properties dialog box.

Viewing Statistics   At any time, select File Properties;
then click the Statistics tab to view a document's
statistics.

After entering any summary information, click OK. Word for
Windows saves the document—along with the summary information you entered—in a file with the name you specified. You are
then returned to the document screen, with the newly assigned
file name displayed in the title bar.

SAVING A NAMED DOCUMENT

Once you have assigned a name to a document, the File Save command saves the current document version under its assigned name; no dialog boxes appear. You can also click the Save button on the Standard Toolbar.

 TIP **Don't Forget!** Save your document regularly as you work on it.

CHANGING A DOCUMENT NAME

You may want to keep the old version of a document under the original name and a revised version under a new name. To change a document name, select File Save As. The Save As dialog box appears showing the current document name in the **File name** text box. Then take the following steps:

1. Change the file name to the desired new name.

2. (Optional) Select a different folder in the **Save in** list to save the document in a different folder.

3. Select OK. Word saves the document under the new name.

CHANGING SUMMARY INFORMATION

You can change the summary information associated with a document at any time. Select File Properties, and the Properties dialog box will appear. Make the desired changes; then select OK. The new information will be registered with the document the next time you save the file.

In this lesson, you learned how to save a document, change a document name, and enter document summary information. In the next lesson, you'll learn how to retrieve a document from a disk.

RETRIEVING DOCUMENTS

In this lesson, you'll learn how to retrieve a document from a disk into Word for Windows, how to search for a specific file, and how to import documents you created with other programs.

RETRIEVING A WORD FOR WINDOWS DOCUMENT

You can retrieve any document created with Word for Windows for further editing, printing, and other functions. To do so, select File Open or click the Open button on the Standard Toolbar. The Open dialog box will be displayed, as shown in Figure 7.1.

 Retrieving a Document This means to reopen a document from your disk into Word for Windows so you can work on it.

 Opening a Document Use File Open to work on a document that you saved earlier.

The file list shows all of the Word documents and folders in the current folder. The Look in box shows the name of the current folder. Here are the actions you can take:

- To open a file, click its name in the list or type its name into the File name box. Then, press Enter or click the Open button.

- To preview the contents of a file, click the file name, then click the Preview button.

- To move up one folder, click the Up One Level button.

- To move down one level to a different folder, double-click the folder name in the file list.

- To move to another folder, open the Look in list and select the desired folder.

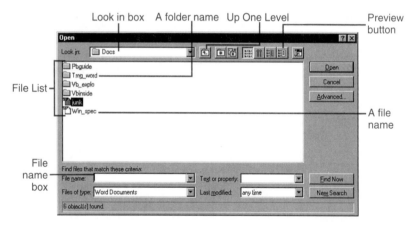

FIGURE 7.1   The Open dialog box.

    Folder   A *folder* is a method of organizing files on a disk. Before Windows 95, folders used to be called *subdirectories.*

To quickly open a file you worked on recently, you can use Word's Recently Used File List. To view this list, select File to display the File menu—the list is displayed at the bottom of the menu just above the Exit command. To open a file on the list, press the number corresponding to the file or click the file name with the mouse. This list displays the document files that you have saved most recently. If you have just installed Word, there will be no files displayed here, of course. If you have saved files and the list still doesn't display, see the next paragraph.

You can control how many files are displayed on the Recently Used File List, and whether or not the list is displayed at all. Select Tools Options to display the Options dialog box, and click the General tab if necessary. Turn the Recently Used File List option on or off to control display of the list. To change the number of files displayed in the list, enter a number in the Entries box, or click the up and down arrows to change the existing entry.

FINDING A FILE

If you cannot remember the full name or location of the file that you want to retrieve, use the Find command in the Open dialog box to find it by name, contents, and/or summary information. When you select the Find Now button, Word for Windows searches for files that meet the criteria you specify in the boxes at the bottom of the Open dialog box:

1. Enter a partial file name in the File name box if you remember part of the file's name. For example, to find all Word documents whose names start with the word SALES, enter the template **SALES***. To search, regardless of file name, leave this box blank.

2. To search for files of a particular type, such as WordPerfect documents, pull down the Files of type list and select the desired file type. Select All Files from this list to search regardless of file type.

3. To find files that contain specified text in the document or summary information, enter the text in the Text or property box. For example, Figure 7.2 shows that the Open dialog box is set up to find files containing the text, *ruler*, before the search began.

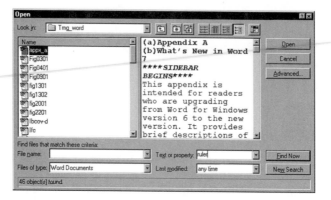

FIGURE 7.2 Using the Open dialog box to find files.

4. To find files based on when they were last modified, pull down the Last modified list and select the desired criterion.

5. Click the Find Now button to start the search. The names of matching files, if any, will be displayed in the file list. Figure 7.3 shows the Open dialog box after performing the search for files containing the text "ruler." You can see that only five documents in the current folder were found.

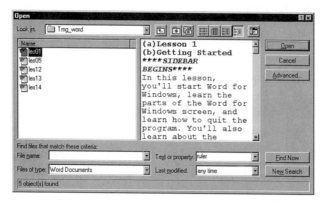

FIGURE 7.3 The Open dialog box displaying the results of a search.

Memory Helper Use the Find Now command to locate a file whose name you've forgotten.

OPENING A DOCUMENT FROM WINDOWS

Most people open documents using the techniques described above: start Word, then use the File Open command to open the document. You can also do things the other way around. If you select the document, Windows knows that it was created with Word and will automatically start Word and load the document. Here's how to do it:

1. Start the Windows Explorer by clicking the Start button on the Windows Taskbar, selecting Programs, then selecting Windows Explorer from the menu that is displayed. If your Desktop includes a shortcut to the Explorer, you can double-click it.

2. In the Explorer window, use the Folders pane to select the desired folder, the one that contains the file you want to open.

3. In the Contents pane, double-click the name of the document file you want to open.

4. Windows will start Word and load the selected document file. If Word is already running, the file will be loaded.

IMPORTING DOCUMENTS

It is possible to import documents that were created with other applications, converting them to Word for Windows format. For example, you can import a document that was created with WordPerfect, therefore, retaining all of its special formatting and fonts. Word for Windows imports from a wide variety of programs. To import a file, follow these steps:

1. Select File Open or click the Open button on the Standard Toolbar. The Open dialog box will be displayed.

2. Pull down the Files of type list and select the type of file you want to import.

3. The File List shows all files of the type shown in the Files of Type box that are located in the current folder. Select the file to import, or type its name directly into the File name box.

4. Select Open.

In this lesson, you learned how to retrieve a document from a disk into Word for Windows, how to search for a specific file, and how to import documents that were created with other programs. In the next lesson, you'll learn how to print your document.

PRINTING YOUR DOCUMENT

In this lesson, you'll learn how to print your document.

QUICK PRINTING

To print a Word for Windows document, you must have installed and selected the printer you are going to use. The printer must be turned on and online. To print the entire document using the current settings:

1. Select File Print, or press Ctrl+P. The Print dialog box appears (see Figure 8.1).

2. Select OK. The document will print.

> **Quick Printing** To print one copy of the entire document without going to the Print dialog box, click the Print button on the Toolbar.

> **Printer Not Working?** Refer to your Microsoft Windows and printer documentation for help.

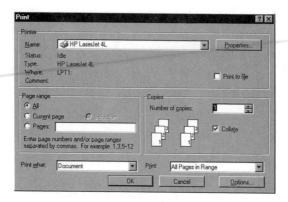

FIGURE 8.1   The Print dialog box.

PRINTING PART OF A DOCUMENT

You can print a single page of a document or a range of pages. This can be useful for checking the results of your editing changes when you've only modified part of the document. Here's how:

1. If you're printing a single page, position the insertion point anywhere on the page that you want to print.

2. Select File Print or press Ctrl+P. The Print dialog box appears.

3. Under Page range, select Current page to print the page where you have placed the insertion point. Select Pages to print a range of pages. Then, enter the beginning and ending page numbers in the box separated by a dash (for example, 2–6).

4. Select OK. The selected page or pages will print. To print noncontiguous pages, enter the page numbers separated by commas (for example: 1, 6, 10).

There are some other options in the Print dialog box that you may find useful:

- To print information from the document other than its text, such as its Summary Information, pull down the Print what list and select.

- To print just the odd or even numbered pages, pull down the Print list and select.

- To print more than one copy, enter the desired number of copies, or click the up and down arrow, in the Number of copies box.

- To print pages in reverse order (last to first), which will produce collated output on printers with face-up output, click the Options to display button and, in the dialog box that is displayed, turn on the Reverse Print Order option.

Two-sided printing? For do-it-yourself, two-sided printing, print the odd numbered pages of your document, place the printed pages in your printer's paper tray, then print the even numbered pages. You'll have to experiment with the paper orientation in the paper tray to get it right.

SETTING UP THE PAGE

By default, Word for Windows formats printer output for 8 1/2-by-11-inch paper in *portrait orientation*. You can modify these settings if needed (if you want to print on 8 1/2-by-14-inch legal paper, for example).

Portrait Orientation This is the default and prints lines parallel to the short edge of the paper. ***Landscape orientation***, by contrast, prints lines parallel to the long edge of the paper.

To change the print orientation and the paper size:

1. Select File Page Setup. The Page Setup dialog box appears.

2. Click the Paper Size tab.

3. Open the Paper Size drop-down box, which lists several common paper sizes.

4. Select the desired paper size.

5. If you select Custom Size from the list, use the **Height** and **Width** boxes to specify the actual paper size.

6. Under **Orientation**, select Portrait or Landscape.

7. Select OK. The new settings will be in effect for your document the next time you print.

PREVIEWING THE PRINT JOB

You can view a screen display that previews exactly what your document will look like when printed. To do this:

1. Select File Print Preview. The current page appears in preview mode (see Figure 8.2).

2. Press PgUp or PgDn, or use the scroll bar to view other pages.

3. Click the Multiple Pages button; then drag over the page icons to preview more than one page at once. Click the One Page button to preview a single page.

4. Pull down the Zoom Control list and select a magnification to preview the document at different magnifications.

5. Click the Print button to print the document.

6. Click Close or press Esc to end Print Preview display.

Print button
    One Page button
        Multiple Pages button
            Zoom Control list

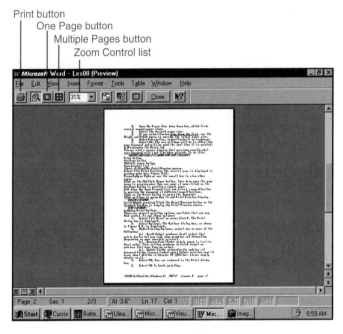

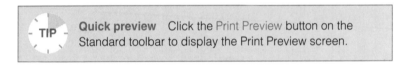

TIP   **Quick preview**   Click the Print Preview button on the Standard toolbar to display the Print Preview screen.

USING PRINT OPTIONS

There are several printing options available that you may find useful. To use these options:

1. Select File Print or press Ctrl+P. The Print dialog box appears.

2. Select Options. The Options dialog box, as shown in Figure 8.3, appears.

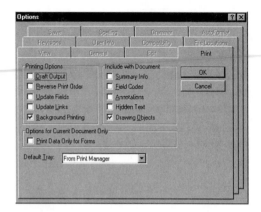

FIGURE 8.3   The Options dialog box.

3. Under Printing Options, select one or more of the
   following:

   - **Draft Output**   Produces draft output that prints
     faster but may lack some graphics and formatting
     (depending on your specific printer).

   - **Reverse Print Order**   Prints pages in last-to-first
     order. This setting produces collated output on
     printers that have face-up output.

   - **Update Fields**   Automatically updates all docu-
     ment fields (except locked ones) before printing.

4. Select OK. You are returned to the Print dialog box.

5. Select OK to begin printing.

In this lesson, you learned how to print your documents. In the
next lesson, you'll learn how to move and copy text.

MOVING AND COPYING TEXT

In this lesson, you'll learn how to move and copy text in your document.

SELECTING TEXT

In Lesson 3, you learned how to select a block of text in order to delete it. You use the same procedures to select text you want to move or copy. Remember, selected text appears on the screen in reverse video.

COPYING TEXT

When you copy text, you place a duplicate of the selected text in a new location. After you copy, the text exists in both the original and new locations. There are several methods available for copying text.

TIP   **Save Your Fingers**   Copying text can save you from having to type. For example, copy a paragraph to a new location when you need to modify it only slightly.

USING THE CLIPBOARD TO COPY

The Clipboard is a temporary storage location offered in Windows programs. You can copy text from one location in your document to the Clipboard and then paste it from the Clipboard to the new location in your document.

1. Select the text you want to copy. The selected text appears highlighted, as shown in Figure 9.1.

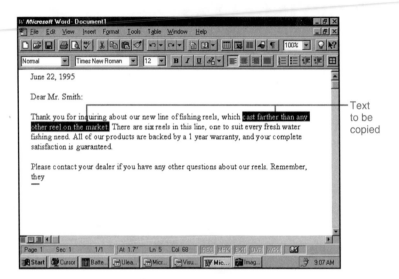

Text to be copied

FIGURE 9.1   Highlighted text to be copied.

2. Select Edit Copy. You can also click on the Copy button on the Toolbar, or press Ctrl+C.

3. Move the insertion point to the new location for the text.

4. Select Edit Paste. You can also select the **Paste** button on the toolbar or press Ctrl+V. The text appears at the new location, as shown in Figure 9.2.

TIP   **Again and Again**   You can paste the same text from the Clipboard more than once. The text remains on the Clipboard, throughout your work session, until you replace it with new text.

Copied text in new location

FIGURE 9.2 The copied text in the new location.

USING THE MOUSE TO COPY

A shortcut for copying is available if you're using the mouse:

1. Select the text to copy.

2. Using the mouse, point at the location where you want the text copied. If necessary, you can first scroll the document to bring the location into view.

3. Press and hold Ctrl+Shift and click the right mouse button. Word copies the selected text to the location you pointed to.

COPYING TEXT THAT YOU JUST TYPED

You can quickly insert a copy of text that you just typed at a different document location:

1. At one document location, type the text that you want to copy.

2. Move the insertion point to the second location for the text.

3. Select Edit Repeat Typing, or press F4.

MOVING TEXT

You can move text from one document location to another. When you move text, Word *deletes* it from the original location and inserts it at the new location.

MOVING TEXT USING THE CLIPBOARD

You can move text with the Clipboard. These are the steps to follow:

1. Select the text to move.

2. Select Edit Cut, click the Cut button on the Toolbar, or press Ctrl+X. Word deletes the selected text from the document and places it on the Clipboard.

3. Move the insertion point to the new location.

4. Select Edit Paste, click the Paste button on the toolbar, or press Ctrl+V. Word inserts the text into the document.

MOVING TEXT WITH THE MOUSE

You can drag selected text to a new location using the mouse. This technique is particularly convenient for small blocks of text.

1. Select the text to be moved. (Figure 9.3 gives an example.)

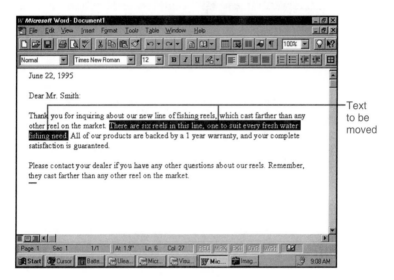

Text to be moved

FIGURE 9.3   To move text, first highlight it.

2. Point at the selected text with the mouse; press and hold the left mouse button.

3. Drag to the new location. As you drag, a dotted vertical line indicates where Word will insert the text.

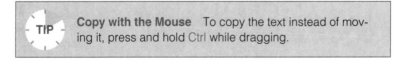

TIP   **Copy with the Mouse**   To copy the text instead of moving it, press and hold Ctrl while dragging.

4. Position the dotted line at the desired insertion point, and release the mouse button. Word moves (or copies, if you were holding Ctrl) the text. (Figure 9.4 shows the new position of the selected text in Figure 9.3.)

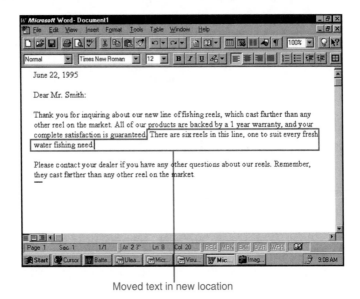

Moved text in new location

FIGURE 9.4   Cut the text and paste it in the new location or drag it to the new location with the mouse.

In this lesson, you learned how to move and copy text. In the next lesson, you'll learn how to format paragraphs.

FORMATTING YOUR DOCUMENT

This lesson introduces you to the concept of formatting (or changing the appearance of) your document and also tells you where to turn for information on specific kinds of formatting.

WHAT IS FORMATTING?

The term *formatting* refers to changes you make in your document's appearance. Whenever you underline a word, set a paragraph off with italics, display a list as a table, or change the page margins you are working with formatting.

Formatting is an important part of many documents. An attractive and well-formatted document has a definite edge on clarity and impact over another document that may have the same content but is poorly formatted. Most of the remaining lessons in this book deal with formatting; this brief lesson serves as a general introduction.

HOW IS FORMATTING APPLIED?

There are two different methods for applying most of Word's formatting commands. The difference depends on whether you want to format text that already exists in the document, or text that you are about to type:

- To format existing text, you first select the text (as you learned in Lesson 3) and then issue the formatting command. The format change affects only the selected text.

- To format new text, move the insertion point to the location where you want the text to appear; then issue the formatting command. The format change will affect new text that you type in.

WHERE DO I TURN NEXT?

If it's possible, I recommend that you continue working through the book's lessons in order. If you need to find information on a particular formatting topic right away, you can refer to this list.

FOR INFORMATION ON...	PLEASE TURN TO...
Using fonts, underlining, boldface, and italics	Lesson 11
Changing the page margins and line spacing	Lesson 12
Using and setting tabs	Lesson 13
Modifying text alignment	Lesson 14
Adding page numbers, headers, and footers	Lesson 17
Creating numbered and bulleted lists	Lesson 22
Arranging text in columns	Lesson 23
Using Word's automatic formatting	Lesson 26
Putting data in tables	Lessons 27

FORMATTING CHARACTERS

In this lesson, you'll learn how to apply special formatting to characters.

WHAT IS CHARACTER FORMATTING?

The term character formatting refers to attributes that apply to individual characters in a document. Font, type size, underlining, italic, and boldface are examples of character formatting. A character format can apply to anything from a single letter to the entire document.

USING FONTS

What Is a Font? The appearance of text is determined—in large part—by its font. A font specifies both the style of text—that is, the appearance of individual characters—and its size. For example, the text you are reading now is printed using the Helvetica font in 9 point size.

The style of a font is denoted by a name, such as Times Roman or Courier. The size of a font is specified in terms of points, with one point equal to 1/72 of an inch. As you enter text in a document, the formatting toolbar displays the font name and point size currently in use. For example, in Figure 11.1, Courier 12 point is the current font.

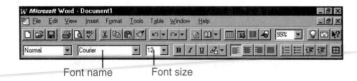

Font name   Font size

FIGURE 11.1   The formatting toolbar displays the name and size of the current font.

CHANGING THE FONT OF EXISTING TEXT

Although the exact fonts and sizes that are available will vary, depending on your Windows installation and the printer you are using, you can change the font style and/or size of any portion of your document. To change font and/or size, follow these steps:

1. Select the text to change. If the selected text currently contains only a single font and size, it displays on the formatting toolbar. If it contains more than one font or size, then none display.

2. To change the font, open the Font Name drop-down box on the formatting toolbar. With the mouse, click the arrow next to the box. On the keyboard, press Ctrl+Shift+F and then press ↓.

3. Select the desired font. With the mouse, click the font name. On the keyboard, use the arrow keys to highlight the name; press Enter.

4. To change point size with the mouse, open the Font Size drop-down box on the formatting toolbar and select the desired point size. On the keyboard, press Ctrl+Shift+P followed by ↓.

TIP

Fast Select!   Remember that you can quickly select an entire document by pressing Ctrl+A.

If you are in Page Layout view or in Normal view with Draft mode off, the screen display will immediately update to show the new font. In Draft mode, different fonts are not displayed on the screen, but the formatting toolbar will display the name and size of the current font. To turn Draft mode on or off, select Tools Options, click the View tab, then click the Draft Font option.

Fast Scroll!   In documents with many different fonts, use Draft display mode to speed up screen scrolling.

CHANGING THE FONT OF NEW TEXT

You change the font that will be used for new text that you type as follows:

1. Move the insertion point to the location where you will type in the new text.

2. Follow the procedures described above for changing the font of existing text (of course, you should not select a block of text).

3. Type the new text. It will appear in the newly specified font. Other text in your document will not be affected.

BOLD, UNDERLINE, AND ITALIC

The attributes boldface, italic, and/or underlining can be applied alone or in combination to any text in your document. These attributes are controlled by the toggle buttons marked **B**, *I*, and U on the formatting toolbar.

Toggle Buttons   These are buttons that, when selected, turn the corresponding attribute on if it is off, and off if it is on.

To apply attributes to new text that you type:

1. Move the insertion point to the location of the new text.

2. Click the Formatting toolbar button(s) for the desired formatting, or press Ctrl+B (bold), Ctrl+I (italic) or Ctrl+U (underlining). On the Formatting toolbar, the button for each attribute that is on appears depressed.

3. Type the text.

4. To turn off the attribute, click the button again or press the corresponding key combination.

To change existing text:

1. Select the text.

2. Click the Formatting toolbar button(s) for the desired formatting, or press Ctrl+B (bold), Ctrl+I (italic) or Ctrl+U (underlining).

In Draft mode, the presence of any character formatting is indicated by underlining. In all other modes, the text appears on-screen with all formatting displayed.

In this lesson, you learned how to format characters. In the next lesson, you'll learn how to set page margins and line spacing.

SETTING MARGINS AND LINE SPACING

In this lesson, you'll learn how to set page margins and line spacing. Word provides default margins and line spacing, but you can easily adjust them to suit your purposes.

SETTING LEFT AND RIGHT MARGINS WITH THE RULER

The Ruler displayed across the top of the Word for Windows work area makes setting margins easy. You can work visually rather than thinking in terms of inches or centimeters. The Ruler is designed to be used with a mouse. To use the Ruler to change margins, you must be working in Page Layout mode (select View Page Layout).

> **TIP** **Displaying the Ruler** If your ruler is not displayed, select View Ruler to display it.

Margin settings made with the Ruler affect the entire document. The white bar on the ruler shows the current margin settings, as shown in Figure 12.1. To change the left or right margin, point at the margin symbol on the ruler, at the left or right end of the white bar (the mouse pointer will change to a two-headed arrow). Then, drag the margin to the new position.

Margins   The left and right margins are the distances, respectively, between the text and the left and right edges of the page.

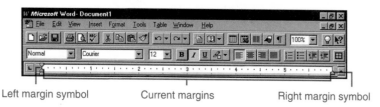

Left margin symbol   Current margins   Right margin symbol

FIGURE 12.1   The ruler displays a white bar showing the current left and right margin settings.

Note that the margin symbols on the ruler are the vertical edges of the white margin bar, *not* the small triangular buttons. These buttons are the indent symbols, which you'll learn about in Lesson 14. If your mouse pointer has changed to a 2-headed arrow, then you know you have found the margin symbol.

 TIP   **Changing Margins**   To change the margins for only a portion of a document, change the left and/or right indent (covered in Lesson 14).

SETTING LEFT AND RIGHT MARGINS WITH A DIALOG BOX

If you prefer not to use the ruler, or want to enter specific values, you can set the left and right margins using a dialog box. This technique also allows you to set the margins for only a part of the document:

1. If you want the new margins to affect only a portion of the document, move the insertion point to the location where the new margin settings should begin.

2. Select File Page Setup, then click the Margins tab to display the Margin options (see Figure 12.2).

3. In the Left box, click the up or down arrows to increase or decrease the left margin. The numerical value is the distance in inches between the left edge of the page and the left edge of text. The sample page in the dialog box shows what the settings will look like when printed.

4. In the Right box, click the up or down arrows to increase or decrease the right margin. The value is the distance between the right edge of the page and the right edge of text.

5. Open the Apply To box and select where the new margins should be used: Whole Document or This Point Forward.

6. Select OK.

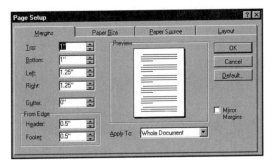

FIGURE 12.2 The Page Setup dialog box with the Margins options displayed.

SETTING TOP AND BOTTOM MARGINS

You also use the Page Setup dialog box to change the top and bottom margins. These margins specify the distance between text and the top and bottom of the page. As with the left and right margins, the top and bottom margin settings affect the entire document.

1. Select Format Page Setup to display the Page Setup dialog box.

2. If necessary, click the Margins tab to display the margins options.

3. In the Top box, click the up or down arrows to increase or decrease the top margin. In the Bottom box, click the up or down arrows to increase or decrease the bottom margin. The sample page in the dialog box shows what the settings will look like when printed.

4. Select OK.

 TIP **Header and Footer Margins** Top and bottom margins do not affect the position of headers and footers.

CHANGING LINE SPACING

Line spacing controls the amount of space between lines of text. Different spacing is appropriate for different kinds of documents. If you want to print your document on as few pages as possible, use single line spacing to position lines close together. In contrast, a document that will later be edited by hand should be printed with wide line spacing to provide space for the editor to write comments.

Word offers a variety of line-spacing options. If you change line spacing, it affects the selected text; if there is no text selected, it affects the current paragraph and text you type at the insertion point. To change line spacing:

1. Select Format Paragraph to display the Paragraph dialog box. If necessary, click the Indents and Spacing tab (see figure 12.3).

2. Pull down the Line Spacing list and select the desired spacing. The Single, 1.5 Lines, and Double settings are self-explanatory. The other settings are:

   - **Exactly:** Space between lines will be exactly the value, in points, that you enter in the At box.

   - **At Least:** Space between lines will be at least the value you enter in the At box; Word will increase the spacing as needed if the line contains large characters.

   - **Multiple:** Changes spacing by the factor you enter in the At box. For example, enter 1.5 to increase spacing by one and a half times, and enter 2 to double the line spacing.

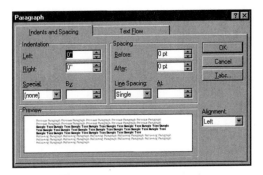

FIGURE 12.3   The Paragraph dialog box with the Indents and Spacing options displayed.

In this lesson, you learned how to set page margins and line spacing. The next lesson shows you how to use and set tabs.

13 SETTING TABS

In this lesson, you'll learn how to use and set tabs.

WHAT ARE TABS?

Tabs provide a way for you to control the indentation and vertical alignment of text in your document. When you press the Tab key, Word inserts a tab in the document, which moves the cursor (and any text to the right of it) to the next tab stop. By default, Word has tab stops at 0.5-inch intervals across the width of the page. You can modify the location of tab stops and control the way that text aligns at a tab stop.

TYPES OF TAB STOPS

There are four types of tab stops; each aligns text differently:

Left-aligned   Left edge of text aligns at tab stop. Word's default tab stops are all left-aligned.

Right-aligned   Right edge of text aligns at tab stop.

Center-aligned   Text is centered at the tab stop.

Decimal-aligned   Decimal point (period) is aligned at tab stop (used for aligning columns of numbers).

Figure 13.1 illustrates the effects of the four tab alignment options. This figure also shows the four different symbols that are displayed on the ruler to indicate the position of tab stops.

Click here until it shows the symbol for the type of tab you want.

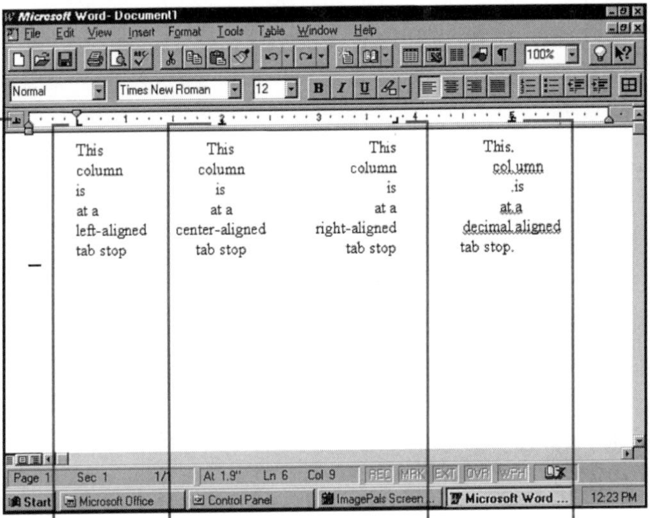

Left-aligned   Center-aligned   Right-aligned   Decimal aligned
tab stop   tab stop   tab stop   tab stop

FIGURE 13.1   The four tab stop alignment options.

CHANGING THE DEFAULT TAB STOPS

You cannot delete the default tab stops, but you can change the spacing between them. Here are the steps to follow:

1. Select Format Tabs to display the Tabs dialog box.

2. In the Default Tab Stops box, click the up or down arrow to increase or decrease the spacing between default tab stops.

3. Select OK.

The default tab stop spacing affects the entire document.

Good-bye Tab   To effectively "delete" the default tab stops, set the spacing between them to a value larger than the page width.

CREATING CUSTOM TAB STOPS

If the default tab stops are not suited to your needs, you can add custom tab stops.

1. Select the paragraphs that will have custom tabs. If no text is selected, the new tabs will affect text that you type at the insertion point.

2. Click the tab symbol at the left end of the ruler until it displays the symbol for the type of tab you want to insert (see Figure 13.1).

3. Point at the approximate tab stop location on the ruler, and press and hold the left mouse button. A dashed vertical line will extend down through the document showing the tab stop position relative to your text.

4. Move the mouse left or right until the tab stop is at the desired location.

5. Release the mouse button.

TIP   If your Ruler is not displayed, select View, Ruler.

When you add a custom tab stop, all of the default tab stops to the left are temporarily inactivated. This ensures that the custom tab stop will take precedence. Custom tab stops' symbols are displayed on the ruler for the paragraph containing the insertion point.

MOVING AND DELETING CUSTOM TAB STOPS

Follow these steps to move a custom tab stop to a new position:

1. Point at the tab stop symbol on the ruler.
2. Press and hold the left mouse button.
3. Drag the tab stop to the new position.
4. Release the mouse button.

To delete a custom tab stop, follow the same steps, but, in step 3, drag the tab stop symbol off the Ruler, then release the mouse button.

USING TAB LEADER CHARACTERS

A tab leader character is a character displayed in the blank space to the left of text that has been positioned using a tab. Typically, periods or hyphens are used for leader characters to create effects such as that shown in Figure 13.2. This menu was created by setting a decimal align tab stop with a dot leader character at the 5.25" position.

To change the leader character for a custom tab stop:

1. Point at the tab stop symbol on the Ruler and double-click. Word displays the Tabs dialog box.
2. Under Leader, select the desired leader character.
3. Select OK.

In this lesson, you learned how to set and use tabs. The next lesson shows you how to indent and justify text.

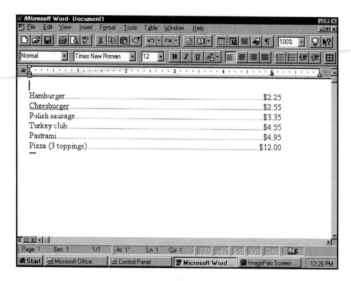

FIGURE 13.2. Using tabs with a leader character.

ALIGNING TEXT

In this lesson, you'll learn how to use indents and justification in your documents. These features help further customize the overall flow and appearance of your text.

INDENTING PARAGRAPHS

Indentation lets you control the amount of space between your text and the left and right edges of the page. Unlike margins, which you learned about in Lesson 12, indentation works for single lines and small sections of text. You can set different indentations for left and right edges, and for the first line of a paragraph.

What Is Indentation? Indentation is the space between the edges of a paragraph and the page margins.

SETTING INDENTS WITH THE RULER

The easiest way to set indents is with the Ruler and the mouse (If your ruler is not displayed, select View Ruler). The Ruler is calibrated in inches from the left margin. The Ruler elements that you use to set indents are illustrated in Figure 14.1.

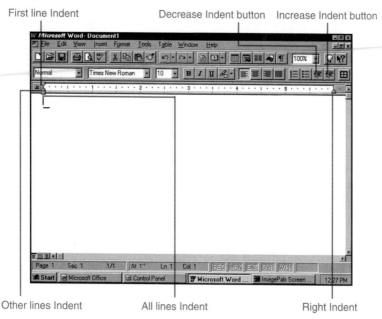

First line Indent Decrease Indent button Increase Indent button

Other lines Indent All lines Indent Right Indent

Figure 14.1. The Ruler can be used to set indentation.

To change indent positions, drag the indent symbols to the desired positions. As you drag, a dotted vertical line is displayed in the document showing the new position.

- To change the indent of the first line of a paragraph, drag the First Line Indent symbol to the desired position.

- To change the indent of all lines of a paragraph, except the first one, drag the Other Lines Indent symbol to the desired position (this is called a hanging indent).

- To change the indent of all lines of a paragraph, drag the All Lines Indent symbol to the desired position.

- To change the indent of the right edge of the paragraph, drag the Right Indent symbol to the desired position.

If you select one or more paragraphs first, the new indents will apply only to the selected paragraphs. Otherwise, the new indents will apply only to new paragraphs that you type from the insertion point forward.

 Quick Indents To quickly increase or decrease the left indent for the current paragraph or selected paragraphs, click the Increase Indent or Decrease Indent button on the Formatting Toolbar.

 Displaying the Formatting Toolbar If the Formatting Toolbar is not displayed, select View Toolbars, then select the Formatting option.

SETTING INDENTS WITH A DIALOG BOX

If you prefer, you can set indents using a dialog box:

1. Select Format Paragraph to display the Paragraph dialog box, then click the Indents and Spacing tab if necessary to display the indents and spacing options (Figure 14.2).

2. Under Indentation, click the up and down arrows in the Left or Right boxes to increase or decrease the indentation settings. For a first line or a hanging indent, select the indent type in the Special pull-down list, then enter the indent amount in the By box. The sample page in the dialog box illustrates how the current settings will appear.

3. Select OK. The new settings are applied to any selected paragraphs or to new text.

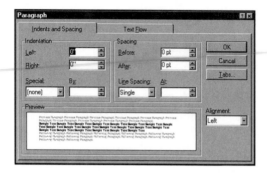

FIGURE 14.2. Setting Indents in the Paragraph dialog box.

JUSTIFYING TEXT

Word for Windows offers four justification options:

- **Left justification** aligns the left ends of lines.

- **Right justification** aligns the right ends of lines.

- **Full justification** aligns both the left and right ends of lines. (This book is printed with full justification.)

- **Center justification** centers lines between the left and right margins.

To change the justification for one or more paragraphs, first select the paragraphs to change; then, click one of the justification buttons on the formatting toolbar, as shown in Figure 14.3.

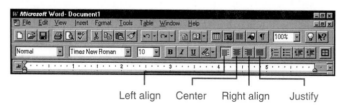

Left align   Center   Right align   Justify

FIGURE 14.3. Click these buttons to set text justification.

What Is Justification? Justification refers to the way in which lines on the page are aligned with the lines above and below them.

If you prefer to use a dialog box to change justification, select the paragraphs and then:

1. Select Format Paragraph to display the Paragraph dialog box.

2. Open the Alignment drop-down box.

3. Select the desired alignment.

4. Select OK.

Changing Justification If you change justification without selecting any paragraphs, then the new justification will apply *only* to any new paragraphs that you type.

In this lesson, you learned how to set indentation and justification in your documents. In the next lesson, you'll learn how to search for and replace text.

15 LESSON

SEARCHING FOR AND REPLACING TEXT

In this lesson, you'll learn how to search for specific text in your document, and how to automatically replace each occurrence of it with new text.

SEARCHING FOR TEXT

You can have Word for Windows search through your document to find occurrences of specific text. For example, you are writing a 40 page report and want to edit the section on the New York Sales Office. You'll quickly find it by searching for "New York." Word's default is to search the entire document. If there is text selected, the search will be limited to the selection.

To search for text, follow these steps:

1. Select Edit Find. The Find dialog box will display, as shown in Figure 15.1.

2. In the Find What text box, enter the text to find. This is the search template.

 Search Template The *search template* is a model for the text you want to find.

3. *(Optional)* Select Find Whole Words Only to match whole words only. With this option off, a search template of *light* would match *light, lightning, lighter,* and so on. With this option on, it would match only *light.*

FIGURE 15.1 The Find dialog box.

4. *(Optional)* Select Match Case to require an exact match for upper- and lowercase letters. If this option is not selected, Word will find matching text of either case.

5. In the Search box, select All to have Word search the entire document. You can also select Down to have Word for Windows search from the insertion point to the end of the document, or from the beginning of the selected text to the end. Select Up to search in the opposite direction.

6. Select Find Next. Word for Windows looks through the document for text that matches the search template. If it finds matching text, it highlights it in the document and stops, with the Find dialog box still displayed.

Now, you can do one of two things:

- Select Find Next to continue the search for another instance of the template.

- Press Esc to close the dialog box and return to the document. The found text remains selected.

If, after searching only part of the document, Word for Windows reaches the start of the document (for an upward search) or the end of the document (for a downward search), you are given the option of continuing the search from the other end of the document. Once the entire document has been searched, a message to that effect is displayed.

FINDING AND REPLACING TEXT

Use the Replace command to search for instances of text, and to replace them with new text. Imagine that you're almost finished with your 400-page novel, and decide to change the main character's name from Brad to Lance. This command will save you a lot of work! The Replace dialog box is shown in Figure 15.2.

FIGURE 15.2   The Replace dialog box.

Make entries in this dialog box as follows:

1. In the Find What text box, enter the target text that is to be replaced.

2. In the Replace With text box, enter the replacement text.

3. If desired, select the Match Case, Find Whole Words Only, and Search options, as explained earlier in this lesson.

4. Select Replace All to have Word for Windows go through the entire document, replacing all instances of the target text with the replacement text. You can also select Find Next to highlight the first instance of the target text.

TIP **Deleting Text**   To delete the target text, leave the Replace With box blank.

If you select Find Next, Word will highlight the first occurrence of the template in the document. You now have three options:

- Select Replace to substitute the highlighted text with the replacement text and then find the next instance of the target text.

- Select Find Next to leave the highlighted text unchanged and then find the next instance of the target text.

- Select Replace All to find and replace all remaining instances of the target text. Use caution, as the Replace All command can be dangerous!

TIP **Saving Time**   To save typing, use abbreviations for long words and phrases. Later, use Replace to change them to final form.

Recovery!   If you make a mistake replacing text, you can recover with the Edit Undo Replace command.

In this lesson, you learned how to search for and optionally replace text. In the next lesson, you'll learn how to use Word for Windows templates.

16 WORKING WITH TEMPLATES

In this lesson, you'll learn how to create and modify templates.

WHAT IS A TEMPLATE?

You learned in Lesson 4 that every Word for Windows document is based on a template, and you also learned how to create a new document based on one of Word's predefined templates. You can also create your own template, or modify existing ones.

CREATING A NEW TEMPLATE

You can create new templates to suit your specific word-processing needs. To create a new template from scratch:

1. Select File New. The New dialog box is displayed.

2. In the dialog box, select the Template option.

3. In the box displaying template icons, be sure that **Blank Document** is selected.

4. Select OK. A blank document-editing screen appears with a default name, such as **TEMPLATE1**.

5. Enter the boilerplate text and other items that you want to be part of the template. Apply formatting to the text as desired; create any styles that you want in the template. (You'll learn about creating styles in Lesson 24.)

6. Select File Save. The Save As dialog box is displayed.

7. In the File name text box, enter a descriptive name up to 256 characters long for the template.

8. Select OK. The template is saved under the specified name and is now available for use each time you start a new document.

 Boilerplate This is text that appears the same in all documents of a certain type.

MODIFYING AN EXISTING TEMPLATE

You can retrieve any existing template from disk and modify it. Then, you can save it under a new name. To modify a template:

1. Select File New to display the New dialog box, shown in Figure 16.1.

2. Select the template that you want to modify. If necessary, select a different folder in the Look In list.

3. Be sure the Template option is selected.

4. Click OK.

5. Make the desired modifications and additions to the template's text and styles.

6. To save the modified template under its original name, select File Save. This is not advised, however. It's better to save the modified template under a new name (see step 7) so the original template will still be available.

7. To save the modified template under a new name (leaving the original template unchanged), select File Save As and enter a new template name.

Note that changes you make to a template are not reflected in documents that were created based on the template before it was changed.

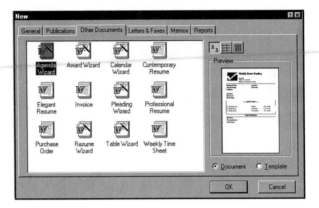

FIGURE 16.1   Opening a template for modification.

CREATING A TEMPLATE FROM A DOCUMENT

To create a template based on an existing Word document you created, follow these steps:

1. Open the document; delete any text and formatting that you do not want to appear in the template.

2. Select File Save As to display the Save As dialog box.

3. Open the Save as Type list and select Document Template.

4. Open the Save in list and select the Template folder.

5. Type the name for the template in the File name box.

6. Select Save.

In step 4, if you don't select the proper template folder, the new template will not be available in Word's New dialog box.

In this lesson, you learned how to create and modify document templates. In the next lesson, you'll learn how to add page numbers, headers, and footers to your documents.

PAGE NUMBERS, HEADERS, AND FOOTERS

In this lesson, you'll learn how to add page numbers, headers, and footers to your documents.

ADDING PAGE NUMBERS

Many documents, particularly long ones, benefit from having numbered pages. Word for Windows offers complete flexibility in the placement and format of page numbers. To add page numbers to your document:

1. Select Insert Page Numbers. The Page Numbers dialog box displays, as shown in Figure 17.1.

FIGURE 17.1 The Page Numbers dialog box.

2. Pull down the Position list and select the desired position on the page: Top of Page or Bottom of Page.

3. Pull down the Alignment list and select Left, Center, or Right. You can also select Inside or Outside if you're printing two-sided pages and want the page numbers positioned near to (Inside) or away from (Outside) the binding.

4. The default number format consists of Arabic numerals
   (1, 2, 3, etc.). To select a different format (for example,
   i, ii, iii), select Format and select the desired format.

5. Select OK.

When you add a page number using the above procedure, Word
for Windows makes the page number part of the document's
header or footer. The next section describes headers and footers.

WHAT ARE HEADERS AND FOOTERS?

A header or footer is text that prints at the top (a header) or bottom (a footer) of every page of a document. A header or footer can
show the page number, or it can contain chapter titles, authors'
names, or any other information you desire. Word for Windows
offers several header/footer options:

- The same header/footer on every page of the document.

- One header/footer on the first page of the document and
  a different header/footer on all other pages.

- One header/footer on odd-numbered pages and a different header/footer on even-numbered pages.

Headers and Footers   The header is at the top of the
page, and the footer is at the bottom.

ADDING OR EDITING A HEADER OR FOOTER

To add a header or footer to your document, or to edit an existing
header or footer, follow these steps:

1. Select View Header and Footer. Word displays the current
   page's header enclosed by a nonprinting dashed line

(Figure 17.2). Regular document text is dimmed, and the Header and Footer toolbar is displayed. On the toolbar, click the Switch button to switch between the current page's header and footer.

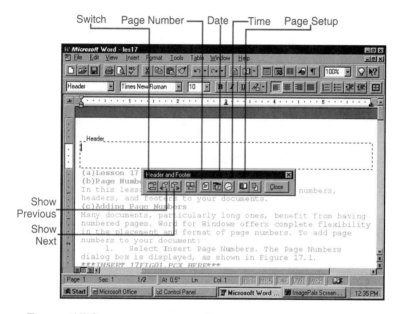

FIGURE 17.2 The Header and Footer Toolbar displayed after selecting View Header and Footer.

2. Enter the header or footer text and formatting using the regular Word editing techniques.

3. If you want the date, time, or page number inserted, click the appropriate button on the toolbar.

4. Click the Show Next and Show Previous buttons on the Header and Footer toolbar to switch between the various sections. As you edit, each header or footer will be labeled (for example, "First Page Header", "Odd Page Footer").

5. When finished, click the Close button on the toolbar to return to the document.

TIP   **Goodbye, header!**   To delete a header or footer, follow the steps above for editing the header or footer. Select all of the text in the header or footer; press **Del**.

CREATING DIFFERENT HEADERS AND FOOTERS FOR DIFFERENT PAGES

Normally, Word displays the same header and footer on all the document's pages. In addition, you have the following options:

- One header/footer on the first page with a different header/footer on all other pages.

- One header/footer on odd-numbered pages with another header/footer on even-numbered pages.

To activate one or both of these options:

1. Select View Header and Footer.

2. Click the Page Setup button on the Header and Footer toolbar. Word displays the Page Setup dialog box. If necessary, click the Layout tab to display the page layout options (Figure 17.3).

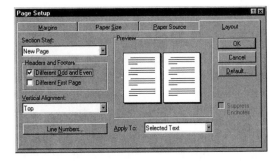

FIGURE 17.3   The Page Setup dialog box.

3. In the Headers and Footers section of the dialog box, turn on the Different Odd and Even option and/or the Different First Page option.

4. Select OK to close the Page Setup dialog box.

In this lesson, you learned to add page numbers, headers, and footers to a document. The next lesson shows you how to use footnotes and endnotes in your documents.

18 FOOTNOTES AND ENDNOTES

In this lesson, you will learn how to use footnotes and endnotes in your documents.

FOOTNOTES VERSUS ENDNOTES

You use footnotes and endnotes to explain, comment on, or provide references for text in your document. A reference mark is placed in the text at the location of the text the note refers to, and the same reference mark is used at the beginning of the corresponding footnote or endnote to identify it. A footnote is positioned at the bottom of the page where its reference mark appears, whereas endnotes are grouped together at the end of the document.

The reference marks for footnotes can be either a symbol, such as *, or sequential numbers. Endnotes are almost always referenced by sequential numbers. Word manages your footnotes and endnotes for you, automatically renumbering them when you delete or insert a note in the document.

INSERTING A FOOTNOTE OR ENDNOTE

These are the steps required to insert a footnote or endnote in your document:

1. Position the insertion point where you want the reference mark located in the text.

2. Select Insert Footnote to display the Footnote and Endnote dialog box (Figure 18.1). Be sure the desired type of note, Footnote or Endnote, is selected.

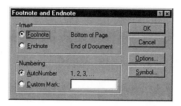

FIGURE 18.1 The Footnote and Endnote dialog box.

3. For sequentially numbered notes, click the AutoNumber option. For a symbol, click the Custom Mark option, then enter the desired symbol in the box. You can also click the Symbol button and select the desired symbol from the dialog box that is displayed.

4. Click the OK button. Depending on which view you are in, one of the following happens:

   • If you are in Normal view, Word opens a pane in which you enter the footnote text; when you are finished, click the Close button.

   • In Page Layout view, you edit the footnote in its actual position on the page. Click the regular document text when you are done.

Quick note keys To insert a footnote, press Alt+Ctrl+F. For an endnote, press Alt+Ctrl+E.

VIEWING AND EDITING NOTES

Editing and viewing footnotes and endnotes is done in the actual note position if you are in Page Layout view, or in a special pane if you are in Normal view. Select Normal or Page Layout from the View menu to change views.

If are in Page Layout View, you can edit and view footnotes and endnotes in the actual note position. Select Page Layout from the View menu to change to Page Layout view. In Normal view you edit footnotes and endnotes in a special pane.

To view a note, select View Footnotes or double-click the note's reference mark in the text. Then, edit the note text using Word's usual editing and formatting commands, including defining and assigning styles and using the Ruler. Click the Close button (if in Normal view) or the regular document text (if in Page Layout view) when you are done editing the note.

MOVING AND DELETING NOTES

To move a note's reference mark to a new location in the text, select either the reference mark alone or with its surrounding text. Then drag it to the new location, or

1. Select Edit Cut, press Ctrl+X, or click the Cut button on the standard toolbar.

2. Move the insertion point to the new location.

3. Select Edit Paste, press Ctrl+V, or click the Paste button on the standard toolbar.

To delete a note, select its reference mark and press Del. When you move or delete a numbered note, Word automatically renumbers the remaining notes.

CUSTOMIZING FOOTNOTES AND ENDNOTES

Word's default settings are to number footnotes with arabic numerals (1, 2, 3...) and endnotes with lowercase Roman numerals (i, ii, iii...). You can change the numbering style of your document's notes as follows:

1. Select Insert Footnote to display the Footnote and Endnote dialog box (shown earlier in Figure 18.1).

2. Click the Options button to display the Note Options dialog box, shown in Figure 18.2.

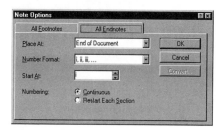

FIGURE 18.2   The Note Options dialog box with the All Endnotes tab displayed.

3. Click the All Footnotes or All Endnotes tab depending on which type of note you are changing the numbering for.

4. Pull down the Number Format list and select the desired numbering style.

5. Click OK to return to the Footnote and Endnote dialog box, then click OK again to return to your document.

In this lesson, you learned how to include footnotes and endnotes in your Word documents. The next lesson covers Word's AutoCorrect feature.

19 USING AUTOCORRECT ENTRIES

In this lesson, you'll learn how to use Word's AutoCorrect feature.

WHAT IS AUTOCORRECT?

The AutoCorrect feature lets you define a collection of commonly used words, phrases, or sentences that can be inserted into a document without typing them each time. You insert an AutoCorrect entry in the document by typing a short abbreviation or name that you assigned to it. Each time you type the abbreviation into the document, the corresponding word or phrase automatically replaces it. Typical uses for AutoCorrect entries are your company name, the closing sentence for a business letter, and your name and title. AutoCorrect can also catch common typographical errors, for example replacing "teh" with "the." An AutoCorrect entry can contain just text or text along with special formatting.

CREATING AN AUTOCORRECT ENTRY

One way to create an AutoCorrect entry requires that you first type the replacement text into your document and add any special formatting that you want included. Then:

1. Select the text for the AutoCorrect entry.

2. Select Tools AutoCorrect. The AutoCorrect dialog box displays (Figure 19.1) with the selected text displayed in the With box.

3. In the Replace box, enter the name or abbreviation that you want to use for the AutoCorrect entry. This should be a short name that describes the entry. You will later use this name when inserting the AutoCorrect entry into documents.

4. Select the Plain Text option to have the AutoCorrect entry inserted as plain text, adopting the formatting of the surrounding text. Select the Formatted Text option to have the AutoCorrect entry's original formatting retained when it is inserted.

5. Select Add.

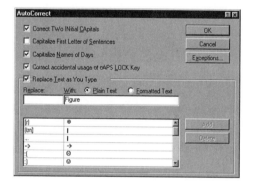

FIGURE 19.1   The AutoCorrect dialog box.

 TIP   **Return Address**   Save time by creating an AutoCorrect entry that contains your name and address.

INSERTING AN AUTOCORRECT ENTRY

Word will automatically insert AutoCorrect entries as you type:

1. Move the insertion point to the location where you want the AutoCorrect entry inserted.

2. Type the name you assigned to the AutoCorrect entry, preceded by a space, and followed by a space or punctuation mark.

3. The corresponding AutoCorrect entry is inserted in place of its name.

You can control whether Word will automatically replace AutoCorrect entries by selecting Tools AutoCorrect. Then, turn the Replace Text as You Type option on or off.

MODIFYING AN AUTOCORRECT ENTRY

You can modify an existing AutoCorrect entry. Such modifications will not affect previous instances of the AutoCorrect entry in your documents.

1. Insert the existing AutoCorrect entry into a document as described earlier in this lesson.

2. Change the text that you just inserted and/or its formatting as desired.

3. Select the newly edited text.

4. Select Tools AutoCorrect. The text you selected will be displayed in the With box. Type the abbreviation to be associated with the modified AutoCorrect entry into the Replace box.

5. Select Replace.

6. When asked whether to redefine the AutoCorrect entry, select Yes.

DELETING AN AUTOCORRECT ENTRY

You can delete an unneeded AutoCorrect entry from the AutoCorrect list. Deleting an AutoCorrect entry does not affect instances of the entry that were inserted previously.

1. Select Tools AutoCorrect.

2. Type the AutoCorrect entry's abbreviation in the Replace box, or select it from the list.

3. Select Delete. The entry is deleted.

In this lesson, you learned how to use AutoCorrect entries. The next lesson shows you how to add symbols and other special characters to your document.

20 SYMBOLS AND SPECIAL CHARACTERS

In this lesson, you'll learn how to use symbols and special characters in your Word documents.

WHAT ARE SYMBOLS AND SPECIAL CHARACTERS?

Symbols and special characters are not part of the standard character set. The Greek letter mu µ and the copyright symbol © are examples. If it's not on your keyboard, Word can probably still display and insert it in your documents.

Which is Which? The distinction between a symbol and a special character is not clear. For example, the Greek mu is considered a symbol, whereas the copyright symbol is considered a special character! There are many more symbols than special characters.

INSERTING A SYMBOL

To insert a symbol at the insertion point, follow these steps:

1 Select Insert Symbol to display the Symbol dialog box. If necessary, click the Symbols tab to display the symbols section, as shown in Figure 20.1.

2. Look through the grid of symbols for the one you want. To see an enlarged view of a symbol, click it.

3. To view other symbol sets, open the Font list and select the desired font.

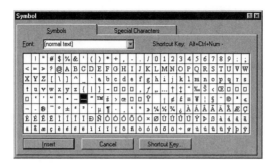

FIGURE 20.1   The Symbol dialog box.

4. To insert the highlighted symbol, select Insert. To insert any symbol, double-click it.

5. Click the Cancel button to close the dialog box without inserting a symbol. Click Close to close the dialog box after you insert a symbol.

INSERTING A SPECIAL CHARACTER

To insert a special character in your document at the location of the insertion point:

1. Select Insert Symbol to display the Symbol dialog box. If necessary, click the Special Characters tab to display the special characters list, as shown in Figure 20.2.

2. Look through the list of special characters for the one you want.

3. To insert the highlighted character, select Insert. To insert any character in the list, double-click it.

4. Click the Cancel button to close the dialog box without inserting a symbol. Click Close to close the dialog box after you insert a symbol.

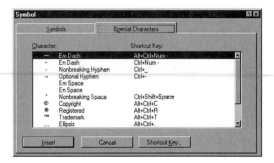

FIGURE 20.2   The Special Characters list.

ASSIGNING SHORTCUT KEYS TO SYMBOLS

If you frequently use a symbol in your document, you may want to assign a shortcut key to it. Then you can insert it quickly by pressing that key combination. Most of the special characters already have shortcut keys assigned to them; you can view these key assignments in the Special Character list.

TIP   **More Shortcuts**   You can also use Word's AutoCorrect feature to quickly insert symbols and special characters. See Lesson 19 for more information.

To assign a shortcut key to a symbol:

1. Select Insert Symbol, then click the Symbols tab, to display the Symbols dialog box (as shown earlier in Figure 20.1).

2. Click the desired symbol. If necessary, first select the proper font from the Font list.

3. If the selected symbol already has a shortcut key assigned to it, the key description displays in the upper right corner of the dialog box.

4. Click the Shortcut Key button to display the Customize dialog box, which is shown in Figure 20.3.

5. Press Alt+N to move to the Press New Shortcut Key box.

6. Press the shortcut key combination that you want to assign. Its description is displayed in the Press New ShortCut Key box.

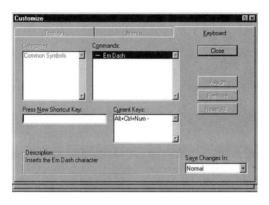

FIGURE 20.3   The Customize dialog box.

7. Under Currently Assigned To, Word displays the name of the symbol, macro, or command that the selected shortcut key is assigned to, or (unassigned) if it has no assignment.

8. If the shortcut key is unassigned, select Assign to assign it to the symbol. If it is already assigned, press BackSpace to delete the shortcut key display and return to step 5 to try another key combination.

9. When done, select Close to return to the Symbols dialog box.

The shortcut keys are really key combinations; you can select from the following (where *key* is a letter key, number key, function key, or cursor movement key):

Shift+*key*

Ctrl+*key*

Alt+*key*

Alt+Ctrl+*key*

Alt+Shift+*key*

Ctrl+Shift+*key*

Ctrl+Shift+Alt+*key*

Using Special Characters

Some of the special characters that Word offers may seem unfamiliar to you, but they can be quite useful in certain documents. The following lists brief descriptions of the less well-known ones.

En dash   A dash that looks slightly longer than the standard dash made with the key above the "P" key on your keyboard. The en dash is properly used in combinations of figures and/or capital letters, as in "Please refer to part 1–A."

Em dash   Slightly longer than an en dash, the em dash has a variety of purposes, the most common of which is to mark a sudden change of thought. For example, "She said—and no one dared disagree—that the meeting was over."

En space   A space slightly longer than the standard space. This space is an en space.

Em space   A space slightly longer than the en space. This space   is an em space.

Non-breaking space   A space that will not be broken at the end of the line. The words separated by a non-breaking space always stay on the same line.

Non-breaking hyphen   Similar to a non-breaking space. That is to say, two words separated by a non-breaking hyphen will always stay on the same line.

Optional hyphen   A hyphen that will not display unless the word it is in needs to be broken at the end of a line.

In this lesson, you learned how to use symbols and special characters in your Word documents. The next lesson covers proofing your document.

21 ## ^{LESSON} PROOFING YOUR DOCUMENT

In this lesson, you'll learn how to use the Word for Windows Speller and Thesaurus utilities to help proof your document.

USING THE SPELLING CHECKER

The spelling checker lets you verify and correct the spelling of words in your document. Word for Windows checks words against a standard dictionary and lets you know when it encounters an unknown word. You then can ignore it, change it, or add it to the dictionary.

To check spelling in a portion of a document, select the text to check. To check the entire document, first move the insertion point to the start of the document by pressing Ctrl+Home. Then:

1. Select Tools Spelling, press F7, or click the Spelling button on the toolbar. Word for Windows starts checking words beginning at the insertion point.

2. If a word found in the document is not in the dictionary, it becomes highlighted in the text and the Spelling dialog box displays (see Figure 19.1).

FIGURE 21.1   The Spelling dialog box.

3. In the Spelling dialog box, the Not in Dictionary box displays the word that was not found in the dictionary. If the spelling checker has found any likely replacements, they are listed in the Suggestions list box. In the dialog box, you have the following options:

- To ignore the highlighted word and continue, select Ignore.

- To ignore the highlighted word and any other instances of it in the document, select Ignore All.

- To change the highlighted word, type the new spelling in the Change To-box or highlight the desired replacement word in the Suggestions list box. Then select Change (to change the current instance of the word) or Change All (to change all instances of the word in the document).

- To add the word to the dictionary, select Add.

4. The spelling checker proceeds to check the rest of the document. When it finishes checking, it displays a message to that effect. To cancel spell checking at any time, select Cancel in the Spelling dialog box.

TIP   **Fast Check!**   To check the spelling of a single word, double-click the word to select it, then press F7.

CHECKING SPELLING AS YOU TYPE

In addition to checking your document's spelling as described above, you can instruct Word to check each word as you type it in. Any word not found in the dictionary will be underlined with a wavy red line, and you can deal with it whenever you choose. To turn automatic spelling checker on or off:

1. Select Tools Options to display the Options dialog box.

2. If necessary, click the Spelling tab.

3. Turn the Automatic Spell Checking option on or off.

4. Click OK.

To deal with a word that has been underlined by Automatic Spell Checking, click the word with the right mouse button. Word displays a pop-up menu containing suggested replacements for the word (if any are found) as well as several commands. Your choices are:

- To replace the word with one of the suggestions, click the replacement word.

- To ignore all occurrences of the word in the document, click Ignore All.

- To add the word to the dictionary, click Add.

- To start a regular spelling check, click Spelling.

 TIP **Hide misspelling marks** If your document contains words underlined by the automatic spelling checker and you want to hide the underlines, select Tools Options, click the Spelling tab, and turn on the Hide Spelling Errors in Current Document option. Turn this option off to redisplay the underlines.

The Thesaurus

A thesaurus provides you with synonyms and antonyms for words in your document. Using the thesaurus can help you avoid repetition in your writing (and also improve your vocabulary). To use the thesaurus:

1. Place the insertion point on the word of interest in your document.

2. Press Shift+F7, or select Tools Thesaurus.

3. The Thesaurus dialog box opens (Figure 21.2). This dialog box has several components:

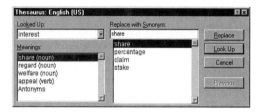

FIGURE 21.2   The Thesaurus dialog box.

- Looked Up displays the word of interest.

- The Meanings box lists alternative meanings for the word. If the word is not found, Word displays an Alphabetical List box instead; this list contains a list of words with spellings similar to the selected word.

- If the Thesaurus finds one or more meanings for the word, the dialog box displays the Replace with Synonym list showing synonyms for the currently highlighted meaning of the word. If meanings are not found, the dialog box displays a Replace with Related Word list

4. While the Thesaurus dialog box is displayed, there are several actions you can take:

- To find synonyms for the highlighted word in the Replace with Synonym list or the Replace with Related Words list (depending on which one is displayed), select Look Up.

- To find synonyms for a word in the Meanings list, select the word and then select Look Up.

- For some words, the thesaurus displays the term Antonyms in the Meanings list. To display antonyms for the selected word, highlight the term Antonyms and then select Look Up.

5. To replace the word in the document with the high-lighted word in the Replace with Synonym list or the Replace with Related Word list, select Replace.

6. To close the thesaurus without making any changes to the document, select Cancel.

TIP   **What does it mean?**   You can use the thesaurus like a dictionary to find the meaning of words you are not familiar with.

In this lesson, you learned how to use the Speller and Thesaurus to proof your document. The next lesson shows you how to create numbered and bulleted lists.

CREATING NUMBERED AND BULLETED LISTS

In this lesson you'll learn how to create numbered and bulleted lists in your document.

WHY USE NUMBERED AND BULLETED LISTS?

Numbered and bulleted lists are useful formatting tools for setting off lists of information in a document; you've seen plenty of both in this book! Word for Windows automatically creates these elements. Use bulleted lists for items that consist of related information, but are in no particular order. Use numbered lists for items with a specific order. Figure 22.1 shows examples of numbered and bulleted lists.

When creating a list, each paragraph is considered a separate list item and receives its own number or bullet.

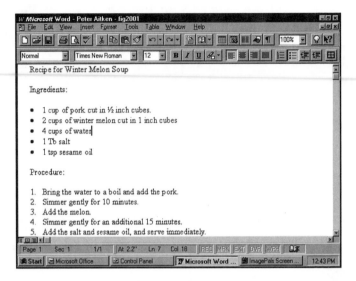

FIGURE 22.1   Word automatically creates numbered and bulleted lists such as these.

CREATING A NUMBERED OR BULLETED LIST

To create a numbered or bulleted list from existing text, follow these steps:

1. Select the paragraphs that you want in the list.

2. Select Format Bullets and Numbering to display the Bullets and Numbering dialog box.

3. Depending on the type of list you want, click the Bulleted tab or the Numbered tab. Figure 22.2 shows the Numbered style options, and Figure 22.3 shows the Bulleted style options.

4. Click the bulleting or numbering option that you want.

5. Select OK.

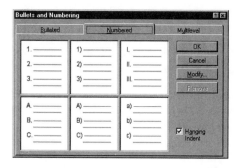

FIGURE 22.2   List numbering style options displayed in the Bullets and Numbering dialog box.

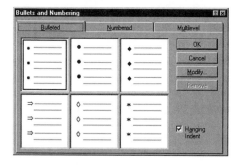

FIGURE 22.3   List bulleting style options displayed in the Bullets and Numbering dialog box.

To create a numbered or bulleted list as you type:

1. Move the insertion point to the location for the list. Press Enter, if necessary, to start a new paragraph.

2. Select Format Bullets and Numbering to display the Bullets and Numbering dialog box.

3. Depending on the type of list you want, click the Bulleted tab or the Numbered tab.

4. Click the bulleting or numbering style that you want.

5. Select OK.

6. Type in the list elements, pressing Enter at the end of each paragraph. Each paragraph will be automatically numbered or bulleted as it is added.

7. At the end of the last paragraph, press Enter. Word will insert an extra, empty list item that will be removed in the next step.

8. Select Format Bullets and Numbering to display the Bullets and Numbering dialog box, then select Remove.

Quick Lists   Create a numbered or bulleted list **TIP** quickly—in the default style—by clicking the Numbered List or Bulleted List button on the Toolbar before typing, or after selecting the list text.

USING MULTILEVEL LISTS

A multilevel list contains two or more levels of bullets or numbering within a single list. For example, a numbered list could contain a bulleted list under each numbered item, or each level could be numbered separately, as in an outline. Here's how to create a multilevel list:

1. Select Bullets and Numbering from the Format menu to display the Bullets and Numbering dialog box.

2. Click the Multilevel tab to display the multilevel options, as shown in Figure 22.4.

3. Click the list style you want, then click OK.

4. Start typing the list, pressing Enter after each item.

5   After pressing Enter, press Tab to demote the new item one level, or Shift+Tab to promote it one level. Otherwise, the new item will be at the same level as the previous item.

6. After typing the last item, press Enter then click the Numbering button on the standard toolbar to end the list.

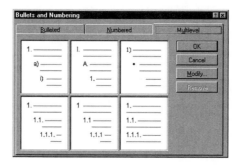

FIGURE 22.4 Use the Multilevel tab in the Bullets and Numbering dialog box to create a multilevel list.

To change the style of an existing multilevel list, or to convert an existing list to a multilevel list:

1. Select all the paragraphs to be in the new list.

2. Select Format Bullets and Numbering, then click the Multilevel tab.

3. Click the desired list style, then click OK.

4. Move the insertion point to each item whose level you want to change.

5. Click the Decrease Indent and Increase Indent buttons on the standard toolbar to change the item's level.

UNDOING A NUMBERED OR BULLETED LIST

Follow these steps to remove bullets or numbers from a list:

1. Select the paragraphs that you want the bullets or numbering removed. This can be the entire list or just part of it.

2. Select Format Bullets and Numbering to display the Bullets and Numbering dialog box.

3. Select Remove.

ADDING ITEMS TO NUMBERED AND BULLETED LISTS

You can add new items to a numbered or bulleted list as follows:

1. Move the insertion point to the location in the list where you want the new item.

2. Press Enter to start a new paragraph. Word automatically inserts a new bullet or number, and renumbers the list items as needed.

3. Type in the new text.

4. If it's a multilevel list, click the Decrease Indent and Increase Indent buttons on the standard toolbar to change the item's level, if desired.

5. Repeat as many times as needed.

This lesson showed you how to create numbered and bulleted lists. The next lesson shows you how to arrange text in columns.

ARRANGING TEXT IN COLUMNS

In this lesson you'll learn how to use columns in your documents.

WHY USE COLUMNS?

Columns are commonly used in newsletters, brochures, and similar documents. The shorter lines of text provided by columns are easier to read, and also provide greater flexibility in formatting a document with graphics, tables, and so on. Word for Windows makes it easy to use columns in your documents. Figure 23.1 shows a document formatted with three columns.

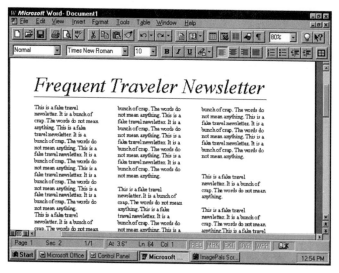

FIGURE 23.1 A document formatted with three columns.

Note that the Word for Windows columns feature creates *newspaper* style columns, in which the text flows to the bottom of one column and then continues at the top of the next column on the page. For side-by-side paragraphs, such as you would need in a résumé or a script, use Word's table feature, covered in Lesson 27.

CREATING COLUMNS

Word for Windows has four predefined column layouts:

- Two equal width columns
- Three equal width columns
- Two unequal width columns with the wider column on the left
- Two unequal width columns with the wider column on the right

You can apply any of these column formats to all or part of a document, to selected text, or from the insertion point onward. Follow these steps:

1. If you want only a part of the document in columns, select the text that you want in columns, or move the insertion point to the location where you want columns to begin.

2. Select Format Columns to display the Columns dialog box (Figure 23.2).

3. Under Presets, click the column format that you want.

4. Pull down the Apply To list and specify the extent to which the columns should apply.

5. Turn on the Line Between option to display a vertical line between columns.

6. Select OK.

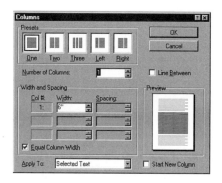

FIGURE 23.2 The Columns dialog box.

 TIP **Quick columns** To display selected text or the entire document in 1 to 4 equal width columns, click the Columns button on the Toolbar then drag over the desired number of columns.

SCREEN DISPLAY OF COLUMNS

To view columns on-screen while you are editing, you must be working in Page Layout mode. In Normal mode, Word displays only a single column at a time (although your columns will be printed). To switch to Page Layout mode, select View Page Layout.

MODIFYING COLUMNS

Here are the steps to follow to modify existing columns:

1. Select the text in columns that you want to modify.

2. Select Format Columns to display the Columns dialog box. The options in the dialog box will reflect the current settings for the selected columns.

3. Make changes to the column settings as desired.

4. Select OK.

TURNING COLUMNS OFF

To convert multiple column text back to normal one column text, follow these steps:

1. Select the text that you want to change from multiple to a single column.

2. Select Format Columns to display the Columns dialog box.

3. Under Presets, select the One style option.

4. Select OK.

This lesson showed you how to arrange text in columns. The next lesson shows you how to use styles.

USING STYLES

In this lesson, you'll learn how to use styles in your documents.

UNDERSTANDING STYLES

A style is a collection of formatting specifications that has been assigned a name and saved. A style could contain, for example, specifications for font name and size, attributes such as underlining and italic, indentation, and line spacing. You can quickly apply a style to any text in any Word for Windows document. Affixing a style is a lot faster than manually applying each individual formatting element, and has the added advantage of assuring consistency. If you later modify a style's formatting, all text in the document to which that style has been assigned will automatically change to reflect the new style definition. Every paragraph in a Word document has a paragraph style applied to it; the default style is Word's predefined Normal style.

 What Is a Style? A *style* is a named grouping of paragraph and character formatting that can be reused.

Word has two types of styles:

- *Paragraph* styles apply to entire paragraphs, and can include all aspects of formatting that affect a paragraph's appearance: font, line spacing, indents, tab stops, borders, and so on.

- *Character* styles apply to any section of text, and can include any formatting that applies to individual characters–font name and size, underlining, boldface, etc.–in other words, any of the formats that are assigned via the Font command on the Format menu.

The formatting of character styles is applied in addition to whatever formatting the text already possesses. For example, if you apply a character style defined as boldface to a word in a sentence that is already formatted as italics, the word will display in bold italics.

Word for Windows comes with several predefined paragraph and character styles. You can use these styles as-is, or modify them to suit your needs and create your own new styles. These topics are covered in this lesson and the next lesson.

VIEWING STYLE NAMES

The Style box at the left end of the Formatting Toolbar displays the current style name–that is, the name of the style assigned to the text where the insertion point is located. If there is text selected or if the insertion point is in text that has a character style applied, then the Style box displays the character style name. Otherwise it displays the paragraph style of the current paragraph.

Every paragraph in a Word document has a paragraph style applied to it; the default style is Word's predefined Normal style.

Word for Windows can also display the name of the paragraph style assigned to each paragraph in your document. The style names are displayed in a column along the left margin of the screen. This is shown in Figure 24.1.

To display the style name area:

1. Select Tools Options, then if necessary click the View tab to display the view options.

2. In the Window section, find the Style Area Width box. This box displays the width of the area at the left of the screen where the style names are displayed. Click the up arrow, or type in a number, to set a positive width for the style name area. A setting of 0.5" is good for most situations. To hide the style name area, enter a width of 0.

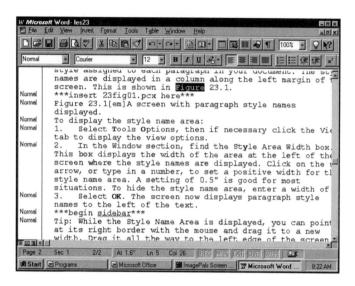

FIGURE 24.1   A screen with paragraph style names displayed.

3. Select OK. The screen displays paragraph style names to the left of the text.

Quick Adjustment   While the Style Name Area is displayed, you can point at its right border with the mouse and drag it to a new width. Drag it all the way to the left edge of the screen to hide the style area.

ASSIGNING A STYLE

To assign a style to text:

1. To assign a paragraph style to multiple paragraphs, select the paragraphs. To assign the style to a single paragraph, place the insertion point anywhere inside the paragraph. To assign a character style, select the text that you want the style to affect.

2. Open the Style drop-down box on the Formatting Toolbar. With the mouse, click the arrow next to the box. With the keyboard, press Ctrl+Shift+S and then press ⬇. The Style box appears, listing all available styles (see Figure 24.2).

FIGURE 24.2   You select a style from the Style box on the Formatting Toolbar.

3. Select the desired style. With the mouse, click the style name. With the keyboard, use the arrow keys to highlight the style name, and then press Enter.

4. The style is applied to the specified text.

Which Kind of Style?   In the Style box, paragraph styles are listed with the paragraph symbol next to them, and character styles are listed with an underlined letter "a" next to them.

Removing a Style   To remove a character style from text, select the text and apply the character style, "Default Paragraph Font."

In this lesson, you learned how to use paragraph and character styles to format your document. The next lesson shows you how to create your own styles.

CREATING AND MODIFYING STYLES

In this lesson, you'll learn how to create your own styles, and how to modify existing styles.

CREATING A NEW STYLE

You are not limited to using Word's predefined styles. In fact, you can create new paragraph and character styles to suit your own specific needs. Follow these steps to create a new paragraph style:

1. Find a paragraph that you want the new style applied to.

2. Format the paragraph as desired–in other words, with the formatting that you want included in the style definition.

3. With the insertion point anywhere in the paragraph, activate the Style box by clicking it or by pressing Ctrl+Shift+S.

4. Type in the new style name and press Enter.

In step 4, be sure not to enter the name of an existing style. If you do, that style's formatting will be applied to the paragraph and the formatting changes that you made will be lost. If this happens, you can recover the formatting by issuing the Edit Undo command.

Here's how to create a new character style:

1. Select Format Style to display the Style dialog box.

2. In the dialog box select New. The New Style dialog box is displayed (Figure 25.1).

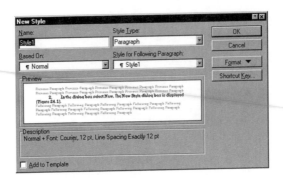

FIGURE 25.1 The New Style dialog box.

3. Pull down the Style Type list and select Character.

4. Select the Name box and type in the name for the new style.

5. Pull down the Format list and select Font. Word displays the Font dialog box.

6. Specify the character formatting that you want in the new style, then select OK to return to the New Style dialog box.

7. Select OK, then select Close.

MODIFYING A STYLE

You can change the formatting associated with any paragraph style. When you do so, all text in the document that has the style assigned will be modified. Here's how:

1. To modify a paragraph style, select a paragraph formatted with the style. To modify a character style, select text (at least one character) that has that style assigned. The style name will be displayed in the Style box on the ribbon.

2. Make the desired changes to the text's formatting.

3. Be sure that the original text or paragraph is still selected.

4. Click the Style box on the Formatting Toolbar, and then click anywhere in the document window.

5. Word for Windows displays the Reapply Style dialog box. Be sure that the Redefine the style using the selection as an example? option is selected.

6. Select OK. The style is redefined with the new formatting.

MODIFYING STYLES—ANOTHER METHOD

Here's an alternative for modifying existing styles:

1. Select Format Style to display the Style dialog box, which is shown in Figure 25.2.

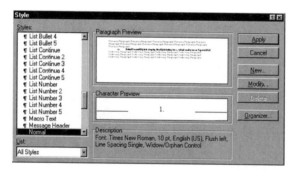

FIGURE 25.2   The Style dialog box.

Quick style   Press Ctrl+Shift+S twice to display the Style dialog box.

2. In the Styles list, highlight the name of the style you want to modify.

3. Select Modify to display the Modify Style dialog box.

4. Select Format. From the displayed list, select the type of formatting you want to modify. The number of formatting types available on the list depends on whether you modify a Paragraph style or a Character style.

5. Word displays the appropriate formatting dialog box. Make the desired changes, then select OK. You return to the Modify Style dialog box.

6. Repeat steps 4 and 5 as many times as needed to make all the desired modifications to the style's formatting.

7. From the Modify Styles dialog box, select OK. You return to the Style dialog box.

8. Select Apply if you want to apply the newly modified style. Select Close to return to the document without applying the style. In either case, all text in the document that has been assigned that style will automatically be reformatted with the modifications you just made.

In this lesson, you learned how to create and modify styles. The next lesson shows you how to use automatic formatting.

Using Automatic Formatting

In this lesson you'll learn how to have Word automatically format your document.

What is Automatic Formatting?

Automatic Formatting refers to Word's ability to analyze the structure of a document and recognize certain common elements, such as body text, headings, bulleted lists, and quotations. Word will then apply appropriate styles to the various text elements to create an attractively formatted document (for more information on styles, please refer to Lessons 24 and 25). You can accept or reject all or part of the automatically applied format, and can later make any desired modifications to the document. In addition to applying styles, Automatic Formatting can remove extra "returns" between paragraphs, create bulleted lists, and more.

Is automatic formatting right for you? You'll have to try it out to find out. Take a document that characterizes one you usually work on, save it under a new name (so the original is not changed) and experiment. You'll soon find out whether you like automatic formatting, or whether you prefer manual application.

Applying Automatic Formatting

You can apply automatic formatting to all or part of a document:

1. To format part of a document, select the text. To format the entire document, the insertion point can be anywhere in the document.

2. Select Format AutoFormat, then select OK. Word analyzes and reformats the document, and displays the AutoFormat dialog box, shown in Figure 26.1.

Figure 26.1   Use the AutoFormat dialog box to accept or reject the formatting applied by the AutoFormat command.

3. Use the vertical scroll bar to scroll through the document and examine the new formatting. The dialog box will remain displayed; grab its title bar and drag it to another location if it is blocking your view of the document.

4. Select Reject All to undo all formatting changes and return the document to its original state. Select Accept to accept all the changes. Select Review Changes if you want to review the changes and accept or reject them individually (see below).

Reviewing the Formatting Changes

If you select Review Changes in step 4 above, you can scroll through the document and examine each individual formatting change, then either accept it or reject it. The Review AutoFormat Changes dialog box will be displayed during this procedure, as shown in Figure 26.2. Scroll through the document using the vertical scroll bar; Word indicates the changes that were made using the following marks, as listed in Table 26.1. These marks also appear in the document in Figure 26.2.

TABLE 26.1   WORD INDICATES FORMATTING CHANGES MADE

CHANGE MADE	MARK DISPLAYED
New style applied to the paragraph	Blue paragraph mark
Paragraph mark deleted	Red paragraph mark
Text or spaces deleted	Strikethrough
Characters added	Underline
Text or formatting changed	Vertical bar in left margin

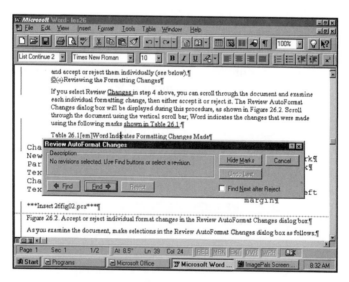

FIGURE 26.2   Accept or reject individual format changes in the Review AutoFormat Changes dialog box.

As you examine the document, make selections in the Review AutoFormat Changes dialog box as follows:

- Select Find → or ← Find to highlight the next or previous change.

- Select Reject to undo the highlighted change.

- Select Undo Last to reverse the last Reject command (restoring the rejected change).

- Select Hide Marks to display the document as it would appear if all remaining changes are accepted. Select Show Marks to return to revisions display.

- Turn on the Find Next After Reject option to have Word automatically find the next revision after you reject the current one.

- Select Close to accept the remaining revisions and return to the AutoFormat dialog box.

Setting the AutoFormat Options

The AutoFormat feature has a number of settings that control which document elements it will modify. You can change these options to suit your preferences:

1. Select Tools Options to display the Options dialog box.

2. Click the AutoFormat tab to display the AutoFormat options (Figure 26.3).

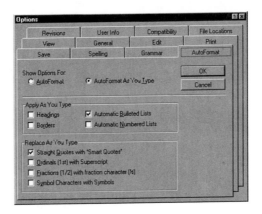

Figure 26.3 Use the Options dialog box to set Word's AutoFormat options.

3. Under Show Options For, select AutoFormat.

4. Turn options on or off to control which document elements the AutoFormat command will affect.

5. Select OK.

AUTOFORMATTING AS YOU TYPE

The first part of this chapter showed you how Word automatically formats an existing document. Word can also format certain elements of your text as you type them. For example, if you start a line with a dash and a space, Word interprets it as being the start of a bulleted list and formats it accordingly. To control which aspects of "format as you type" are active, follow these steps:

1. Select Tools Options to display the Options dialog box. If necessary, click the AutoFormat tab in the dialog box.

2. Under Show Options For, select Autoformat as You Type.

3. Turn options on or off to control the formatting that will be applied as you type.

4. Select OK.

This lesson showed you how to use Word's automatic formatting capability. In the next lesson you'll learn how to use tables.

27 TABLES

In this lesson, you'll learn how to add tables to your documents.

USES FOR TABLES

A *table* lets you organize information in a row and column format. Each entry in a table, called a *cell,* is independent of all other entries. You can have almost any number of rows and columns in a table. You also have a great deal of control over the size and formatting of each cell. A table cell can contain anything that a Word document can contain except another table–text, graphics, and so on.

TIP

Why Tables? Use tables for columns of numbers, lists, and anything else that requires a row and column arrangement.

INSERTING A TABLE

You can insert a new, empty table at any location within your document. Just follow these steps:

1. Move the insertion point to where you want the table.

2. Select Table Insert Table. The Insert Table dialog box, as shown in Figure 27.1, is displayed.

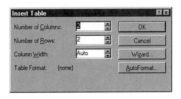

FIGURE 27.1 The Insert Table dialog box.

3. If you want to use the Table Wizard to create your table, click the Wizard button. Lesson 4 showed you how to use Wizards. Otherwise, continue with the next step.

4. In the Number of Columns and Number of Rows boxes, click the arrows or enter the number of rows and columns the table should have. (You can adjust these numbers later if you wish.)

5. In the Column Width box, select the desired width for each column, in inches. Select Auto in this box to have the page width evenly divided among the specified number of columns.

6. Select OK. A blank table is created with the insertion point in the first cell. Figure 27.2, for example, shows a blank table with 4 rows and 3 columns.

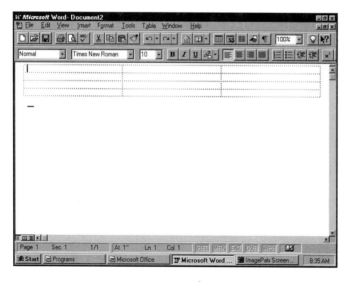

FIGURE 27.2   A blank table with 4 rows and 3 columns.

Quick Tables   To quickly insert a table, click the Table button on the Standard Toolbar, then drag over the desired number of rows and columns.

WORKING IN A TABLE

When the insertion point is in a table cell, you can enter and edit text as you would in the rest of the document. Text entered in a cell automatically wraps to the next line within the column width. Navigate in a table using the special key combinations listed below:

PRESS THIS	To
Tab	Move to the next cell in a row.
Shift+Tab	Move to the previous cell in a row.
Alt+Home	Move to the first cell in the current row.
Alt+PgUp	Move to the top cell in the current column.
Alt+End	Move to the last cell in the current row.
Alt+PgDn	Move to the last cell in the current column.

If the insertion point is at the edge of a cell, you can also use the arrow keys to move between cells.

EDITING AND FORMATTING A TABLE

Once you've created a table and entered some information, you can edit its contents and format its appearance to suit your needs.

DELETING AND INSERTING CELLS, ROWS, AND COLUMNS

You can delete individual cells, erasing their contents and leaving a blank cell. You can also delete entire rows and columns. When you do so, columns to the right or rows below move to fill in for the deleted row or column.

Fast Select! To select an entire cell, click in the left margin of the cell, between the text and the cell border. The mouse pointer changes to an arrow when it's in this area.

To delete the contents of a cell:

1. Select the cell.

2. Press Del.

To delete an entire row or column:

1. Move the insertion point to any cell in the row or column to be deleted.

2. Select Table Delete Cells. A dialog box is displayed (see Figure 27.3).

FIGURE 27.3 The Delete Cells dialog box.

3. In the dialog box, select Delete Entire Row or Delete Entire Column.

4. Select OK. The row or column is deleted.

To insert a single row or column:

1. Move the insertion point to a cell to the right of where you want the new column or below where you want the new row.

2. Select Table Insert Columns to insert a new, blank column to the left of the selected column. Select Table Insert Rows to insert a new, blank row above the selected row.

 It Varies! The commands on the Table menu change according to circumstances. For example, if you have selected a column in a table, the Insert Columns command is displayed but the Insert Rows command is not.

To insert more than one row or column:

1. Select cells that span the number of rows or columns you want to insert. For example, to insert three new rows between rows 2 and 3, select cells in rows 3, 4, and 5 (in any column).

2. Select Table Select Row (if inserting rows) or Table Select Column (if inserting columns).

3. Select Table Insert Rows or Table Insert Columns, as appropriate.

To insert a new row at the bottom of the table:

1. Move the insertion point to the last cell in the last row of the table.

2. Press Tab. A new row is added at the bottom of the table.

To insert a new column at the right edge of the table:

1. Click just outside the table's right border.

2. Select Table Select Column.

3. Select Table Insert Columns.

MOVING OR COPYING COLUMNS AND ROWS

Here's how to copy or move an entire column or row from one location in a table to another.

1. Select the column or row.

2. To copy, press Ctrl+C or click the Copy button on the Standard Toolbar. To move, press Ctrl+X or click the Cut button.

3. Move insertion point to the new location for the column or row. It will be inserted above or to the left of the location of the insertion point.

4. Press Ctrl+C or click the Paste button on the Standard Toolbar.

CHANGING COLUMN WIDTH

You can quickly change the width of a column with the mouse:

1. Point at the right border of the column whose width you want to change. The mouse pointer changes to a pair of thin vertical lines with arrowheads pointing left and right.

2. Drag the column border to the desired width.

You can also use a dialog box to change column widths:

1. Move the insertion point to any cell in the column you want to change.

2. Select Table Cell Height and Width. The Cell Height and Width dialog box is displayed (see Figure 27.4). If necessary, click the Column tab to display the column options.

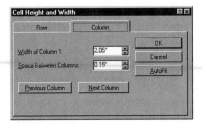

FIGURE 27.4 The Cell Height and Width dialog box, with the Column tab showing.

3. In the Width of Column box, type in the desired column width, or click the up and down arrows to change the setting. To automatically adjust the column width to fit the widest cell entry, click the Autofit button.

4. Change the value in the Space Between Columns box to modify spacing between columns.

5. Click Next Column or Previous Column to change the settings for other columns in the table.

6. Select OK. The table changes to reflect the new column settings.

AUTOMATIC TABLE FORMATTING

The AutoFormat command makes it a snap to apply attractive formatting to any table:

1. Place the insertion point anywhere in the table.

2. Select Table Table AutoFormat. The Table AutoFormat dialog box is displayed (Figure 27.5).

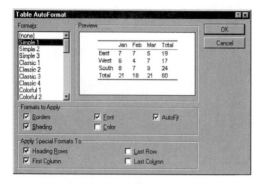

FIGURE 27.5 Use the Table AutoFormat dialog box to apply table formatting.

3. The Formats box lists the available table formats. As you scroll through the list, the Preview box shows the appearance of the highlighted format.

4. In the lower section of the dialog box are a number of formatting options. Select and deselect options as needed until the preview shows the table appearance you want.

5. Select OK. The selected formatting is applied to the table.

In this lesson, you learned how to add tables to your documents. In the next lesson, you'll learn how to add graphics to your documents.

28 ADDING GRAPHICS TO YOUR DOCUMENT

In this lesson, you'll learn how to add graphics to your documents.

ADDING A GRAPHICS IMAGE

A graphics image is a picture that is stored on disk in a graphics file. Word for Windows can utilize graphics files created by a wide variety of applications, including Lotus 1-2-3, Windows Metafiles, Micrografx Designer, and AutoCAD. Additionally, your Word installation includes a small library of clip art images that you can use in your documents. Figure 28.1 shows a document with a graphic image.

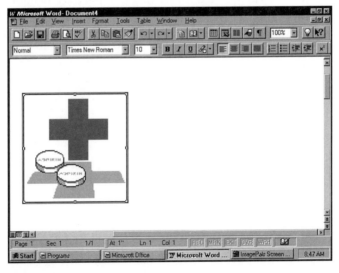

FIGURE 28.1 A document with a displayed graphic.

To add a graphics image to a Word for Windows document, follow these steps:

1. Move the insertion point to the location for the graphic.

2. Select Insert Picture. The Insert Picture dialog box, shown in Figure 28.2, is displayed.

3. If necessary, pull down the Look inlist to specify the folder where the graphics file is located.

4. The large box in the center of the dialog box normally lists all graphics files in the specified directory. To have the list restricted to certain types of graphics files, open the Files of type list and select the desired file type.

5. In the File name box, type the name of the file to insert, or select the file name from the list.

6. To preview the picture in the Preview box (as shown in Figure 28.2), click the Previewbutton.

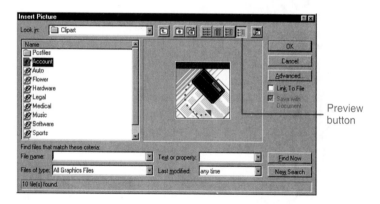

Preview button

FIGURE 28.2   The Insert Picture dialog box.

7. Select the Link To File option if you want the graphic in your document updated if the graphics file on disk changes.

8. Select OK. The graphic is inserted into your document.

DISPLAYING GRAPHICS

The display of graphics images can slow down screen scrolling. If you're working on the document text and don't need to see the images, you can speed up screen display by displaying empty rectangles called *placeholders* in place of the images. In addition, if you selected the Link To File option when inserting the graphic file, Word for Windows inserts a field code in the document. The screen will display this code instead of the picture when field codes are displayed. Here's how to control the display of graphics:

1. Select Tools Options to display the Options dialog box.

2. If necessary, click the View tab to display the View options.

3. In the Show section, turn the Picture Placeholders and Field Codes options on or off as desired.

4. Select OK.

The screen display of placeholders or field codes does not affect printing, which will always include the actual graphics.

 Fast Takes   When working on a document that contains a lot of graphics, you can speed up screen display and scrolling by displaying placeholders for the graphics.

SELECTING A GRAPHIC

Before you can work with a graphic in your document, you must select it:

- With the mouse, click the graphic.

- With the keyboard, position the insertion point immediately to the left of the graphic, and then press Shift+→.

When a graphic is selected, it is surrounded by eight small black squares called *sizing handles*.

CROPPING AND RESIZING A GRAPHIC

You can resize a graphic in your document, displaying the entire picture at a different size. You can also crop a graphic, hiding portions of the picture that you don't want to display. To resize or crop a graphic:

1. Select the graphic.

2. Point at one of the resizing handles. The mouse pointer will change to a double-headed arrow.

3. To resize, press the left mouse button and drag the handle until the outline of the graphic is at the desired size. You can either enlarge or shrink the graphic.

4. To crop, press and hold Shift, then press the left mouse button and drag a handle toward the center of the graphic.

5. Release the mouse button.

DELETING, MOVING, AND COPYING GRAPHICS

To delete a graphic, select it and press Del.

To move or copy a graphic:

1. Select the graphic.

2. Press Ctrl+C or select Edit Copy (to copy the graphic), press Ctrl+X or select Edit Cut (to move the graphic). You can also click the Copy or Cut button on the Toolbar.

3. Move the insertion point to the new location for the graphic.

4. Press Ctrl+V, or click the Paste button on the Toolbar.

In this lesson, you learned how to add graphics to your documents. The next lesson shows you how to open multiple documents.

29 LESSON

OPENING MULTIPLE DOCUMENTS

In this lesson, you'll learn how to open multiple documents in Word for Windows.

WHY USE MULTIPLE DOCUMENTS?

You may feel that working on one document at a time is quite enough. In some situations, however, the ability to work on multiple documents at the same time can be very useful. You can refer to one document while working on another, and you can copy and move text from one document to another. Essentially, Word for Windows can have an unlimited number of documents open, simultaneously.

STARTING A NEW DOCUMENT

You can start a new document while you're working on an existing document. To do so, follow the procedures you learned in Lesson 3 for creating a new document. Briefly:

- To create a new document based on the Normal template, click the New button on the Standard toolbar.

- To create a document based on another template or one of Word's Wizards, select File New.

OPENING AN EXISTING DOCUMENT

While working in one document, you can also open another existing document. Simply select File Open, or click the File Open button on the Standard toolbar and select the name of the document file you want to open (you learned the details of opening documents in Lesson 7). A new window opens and displays the document that you opened. Both the newly opened and the original documents are in memory, and can be edited, printed, and so on. You can continue opening additional documents until all of the files you need to work with are open.

SWITCHING BETWEEN DOCUMENTS

When you have multiple documents open at one time, only one of them can be active at a given moment. The active document is displayed on-screen (although inactive documents may be displayed as well). More important, the active document is the only one affected by editing commands.

To switch between open documents:

1. Select Window. The Window menu lists all open documents. A check marks the name of the currently active document (see Figure 29.1).

FIGURE 29.1 The Window menu, indicating the currently active document.

2. Select the name of the document you want active. You can either click the document name with the mouse, or press the corresponding number key.

3. The selected document becomes active and is displayed on the screen.

> **TIP** **Next Please!** To cycle to the next open document, press Ctrl+F6.

CONTROLLING MULTIPLE DOCUMENT VIEW

Word gives you a great deal of flexibility in displaying multiple documents. You can have the active document occupy the entire screen, with other open documents temporarily hidden. You can also have several documents displayed at the same time, each in its own window. A document window can be in one of three states:

- Maximized: The window occupies the full screen. No other open documents are visible. When the active document maximizes, its title is displayed in Word's title bar at the top of the screen. Figure 29.2 shows a maximized document.

- Minimized: The window is reduced to a small icon displayed at the bottom of the Word screen. The document title is displayed on the icon.

- Restored: The document window assumes an intermediate size, and the document title is displayed in the title bar of its own window instead of Word's title bar.

Figure 29.3 shows both a restored and a minimized document.

Here are the procedures for controlling how multiple documents are displayed:

- To restore or minimize a maximized window, click its Restore or Minimize button.

- To maximize or minimize a restored window, click its Maximize or Minimize button.

- To display a minimized window, click its icon. Then, either click its Restore or Maximize button or select from the pop-up menu that is displayed.

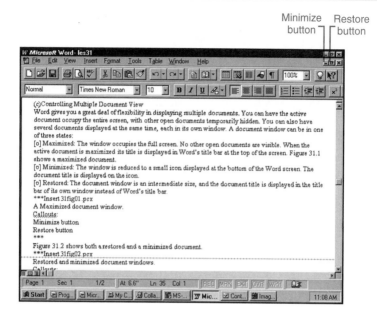

Figure 29.2   A Maximized document window.

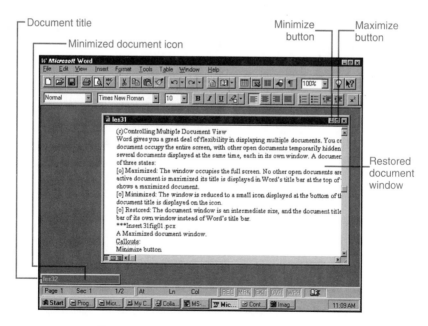

Figure 29.3   Restored and minimized document windows

When a document is in the restored state, you can control the size and position of its window. To move the window, point at its title bar and drag it to the new position. To change window size, point at a border or corner of the window (the mouse pointer changes to a 2-headed arrow), then drag the window to the desired size.

Word offers a command that can be useful when you want to view all of your open documents. Select Window Arrange All to tile all document windows. When you tile your documents, every open document is displayed in a small window with no overlapping. If you have more than a few documents open, these windows will be quite small and won't be very useful for editing. They are useful, however, for seeing exactly what documents you have open and finding the one you need to work on at the moment. Figure 29.4 shows the result of the Arrange All command with 6 documents open.

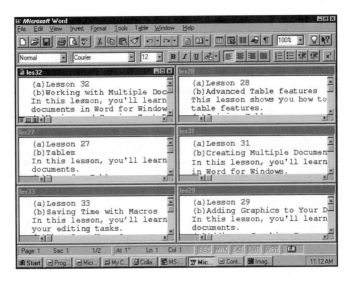

FIGURE 29.4 Six documents displayed with the Arrange All command.

In this lesson, you learned how to open and display multiple documents. The next lesson shows you how to work with multiple documents.

WORKING WITH MULTIPLE DOCUMENTS

In this lesson, you'll learn how to work with multiple documents in Word for Windows.

MOVING AND COPYING TEXT BETWEEN DOCUMENTS

When you have more than one document open, you can move and copy text between documents. These are the procedures to follow:

1. Make the source document active, and select the text that is to be moved or copied.

2. Press Ctrl+X or select Edit Cut (if moving the text), or press Ctrl+C or select Edit Copy (if copying the text). You can also click the Cut and Copy buttons on the Toolbar.

3. Make the destination document active. Move the insertion point to the location for the new text.

4. Press Ctrl+V, or select Edit Paste, or click the Paste button on the Toolbar.

VIEWING TWO SECTIONS OF A DOCUMENT

Sometimes you will be working in a document, particularly a long one, and want to view two different parts of the document. For example, you might want to refer to what you wrote in the Introduction of a report while editing text in the Conclusions. Rather than continually scrolling back and forth, or printing a copy for reference, you can split the document window into two panes and view a different part of the document in each pane. Here's how:

1. Select Windows Split. Word displays a gray horizontal line across your document.

2. Use the mouse or the up arrow and down arrow keys to move the line to the desired position.

3. Click with the mouse or press Enter. The window will split into two panes at the line's position.

4. To remove the split from a window, select Window Remove Split.

When the window splits, each pane has its own vertical scroll bar and Ruler, as shown in Figure 30.1. The text in each pane of a split window scrolls independently. To switch from one pane to the other, click the desired pane. A split window not only lets you view two parts of a document, but also lets you copy and move text from one section to another.

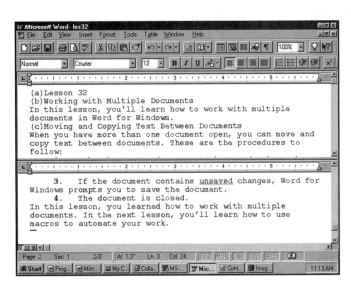

Figure 30.1 A split window, showing two sections of a document simultaneously.

SAVING MULTIPLE DOCUMENTS

When working with multiple documents, save documents with the File Save and File Save As commands that you learned in Lesson 6. These commands will save the active document only. You can save all open documents with a single command, File Save All.

CLOSING A DOCUMENT

You can close an open document once you are finished working with it. To close a document:

1. Make the document active.

2. Select File Close.

3. If the document contains unsaved changes, Word for Windows prompts you to save the document.

4. The document is closed.

In this lesson, you learned how to work with multiple documents. In the next lesson, you'll learn how to use macros to automate your work.

31 SAVING TIME WITH MACROS

In this lesson, you'll learn how to use macros to speed up your editing tasks.

WHAT IS A MACRO?

A *macro* is a sequence of commands and keystrokes that has been recorded and saved by Word for Windows. You can easily play back a macro at any time, achieving the same result as if you had entered each command and keystroke individually. For example, you could create a macro that:

- Converts an entire document from single-spaced to double-spaced.

- Goes through a document and formats the first word of each paragraph in 18 point italics.

- Saves the document to disk and then prints it in draft mode.

 TIP **Why Macros?** Macros save time. By recording frequently needed command sequences as macros, you can save time and reduce errors.

The Word for Windows macro is a complex and powerful feature. The basics you'll learn in this lesson will enable you to create many useful macros.

RECORDING A MACRO

The simplest way to create a macro is to enter the keystrokes and commands yourself while Word for Windows records them. The only operations that Word for Windows cannot record are mouse editing actions. That is, a macro cannot record the mouse moving the insertion point or selecting text; you must use the keyboard for these actions while recording a macro. Other mouse actions, such as selecting menu commands or dialog box options, can be recorded in a macro.

To record a macro:

1. Plan the macro. You should try a procedure out before recording it in a macro to ensure that it works the way you want it to.

2. Select Tools Macro to display the Macro dialog box, which is shown in Figure 31.1

FIGURE 31.1   The Macro dialog box.

3. Type the macro name in the Macro Name text box. The name should describe the actions of the macro. Use any characters except spaces, commas, and periods in the macro name.

4. Select Record to display the Record Macro dialog box (see Figure 31.2).

FIGURE 31.2   The Record Macro dialog box.

5. In the Description box, enter a short description of the macro. Entering a description is optional, but recommended.

6. If the document is based on a template other than **NORMAL**, you can pull down the Make Macro Available To list and select All Documents (if you want the macro available to all documents) or Documents based On... (if you want the macro available only to documents based on the current template).

7. Select OK. Word starts recording the macro. While recording is in progress, Word displays the Macro Toolbar in a corner of the document. Additionally, the REC indicator is displayed in the status line at the bottom of the screen, and the mouse pointer changes to a recorder symbol to remind you to use the keyboard, not the mouse, to select text and move the insertion point (see Figure 31.3).

Stop button ———  ——— Pause button

FIGURE 31.3   Recording is in progress.

8. Execute the actions and commands that you want in the macro. During recording you can click the Pause button on the Macro Toolbar if you want to perform actions that you don't want recorded in the macro. Click Pause again to resume recording. When finished, click the Stop button on the Macro Toolbar to terminate macro recording and store the macro.

TIP   **Quick Start**   Double-click the REC indicator on the status line to start or stop recording a macro.

If you make a mistake while recording a macro, select Edit Undo or press Ctrl+Z to undo the mistake. Then continue recording the rest of the macro as usual.

PLAYING BACK A MACRO

You can play back any macro at any time while you're working on a document, as follows:

1. Select Tools Macro. The Macro dialog box appears (Figure 31.4).

FIGURE 31.4   Choose a macro to run in the Macro dialog box.

2. Type the name of the macro in the Macro Name box, or highlight the name in the list.

3. Select Run. The chosen macro is executed.

Assigning a Shortcut Key to a Macro

If you assign a shortcut key to a macro, you can play the macro back simply by pressing its shortcut key. The shortcut keys are really key combinations; you can select from the following (where *key* is a letter, number, function, or cursor movement key):

Shift+*key*

Ctrl+*key*

Alt+*key*

Alt+Ctrl+*key*

Alt+Shift+*key*

Ctrl+Shift+*key*

Ctrl+Shift+Alt+*key*

To assign a shortcut key to a macro, follow these steps:

1. Select Tools Customize to display the Customize dialog box.

2. If necessary, click the Keyboard tab to display the keyboard options (figure 31.5).

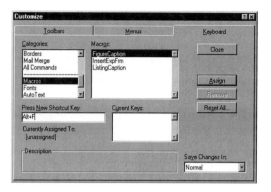

FIGURE 31.5   Use the Customize dialog box to assign a shortcut key to a macro.

3. Scroll through the Categories list until the Macros entry is highlighted.

4. In the Macros list, highlight the name of the macro that you want to assign a shortcut key to.

5. Press Alt+N to move to the Press New Shortcut Key box.

6. Press the shortcut key combination that you want to assign. Its description is displayed in the Press New ShortCut Key box.

7. Under Currently Assigned To, Word displays the name of the macro or command that the selected shortcut key is assigned to, or (unassigned) if there is no assignment.

8. If the shortcut key is unassigned, select Assign to assign it to the macro. If it is already assigned, press BackSpace to delete the shortcut key display and return to step 6 to try another key combination.

9. When done, select Close.

Shortcut Keys   Assign a shortcut key to macros that you will use frequently. To play the macro, simply press the shortcut key while editing the document.

In this lesson, you learned how to use macros to automate your work. This is the last lesson in the book, and you should now be ready to handle just about any word processing task thrown at you. I suggest that you keep this book near your computer so you can refer to it as needed. Don't lend it to anyone—they can buy their own copy!

What's New in Word for Windows 95

This appendix is intended for readers who are upgrading from Word for Windows version 6 to the new version. It provides brief descriptions of features that are new or have changed significantly.

The Latest Word

The basics of Word have not changed. If you were comfortable using Word for Windows Version 6, you'll feel right at home with the latest version. A number of new features, however, bring additional power and convenience to the program. For those features that are covered in this book, you'll find a cross-reference to the appropriate lesson. For more complete information on the new features, click the Contents tab on Word's Help screen, then select the What's New topic.

If you are new to Windows, see Appendix B ("Windows 95 Primer") for a quick introduction.

Opening a Document From Windows

Most people open documents by starting Word, then using the File Open command to open the document. With Windows 95, you can also do things the other way around. If you select the document, Windows knows that it was created with Word and will automatically start Word and load the document. Here's how to do it:

1. Start the Windows Explorer by clicking the Start button on the Windows Taskbar, selecting Programs, then selecting Windows Explorer from the menu that is displayed. If your Desktop includes a shortcut to the Explorer, you can double-click it.

2. In the Explorer window, use the Folders pane to select the desired folder, the one that contains the file you want to open. (See Figure A.1.)

3. In the Contents pane, double-click the name of the document file you want to open.

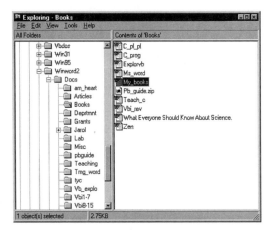

FIGURE A.1   Double-clicking the highlighted document will start Word.

4. Windows will start Word and load the selected document file. If Word is already running, the file will be loaded.

You can also open documents you have worked on recently from the Start menu. Click Start on the Windows Task Bar, then click Documents to display a menu with a list of documents on it. Click the desired document name, and Word will start and load the document. Note that this menu lists all kinds of documents, not just Word documents. You can identify the program that created a document by the icon next to the document name.

ANSWER WIZARD

The Answer Wizard (see Figure A.2) is an addition to Word's Help system. If you are having trouble finding the information you need using the Help Index or Contents, you may want to try the Answer Wizard. It permits you to enter plain English questions, then searches the Help files for the relevant information. Please turn to Lesson 2 for more information on the Answer Wizard.

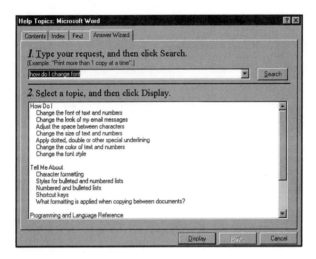

FIGURE A.2   The Answer Wizard searches Help for answers to your plain English questions.

TIP WIZARD

The Tip Wizard (see Figure A.3) is another new part of the Help system. While the Tip Wizard is active, it "watches" what you are doing in your Word document, and displays hints, time saving techniques, and other helpful information. Although the Tip Wizard is aimed primarily at new users, more experienced users may find it helpful also. You'll find more information on the Tip Wizard in Lesson 2.

Automatic Spell Checking

Word has always been able to check the spelling in your documents, but now it can do it as you type. With Automatic Spell Checking (see Figure A.3) enabled, misspelled words are immediately marked in your document, as soon as you enter them. There's more information about Automatic Spell Checking in Lesson 19.

Figure A.3   The Tip Wizard offers plain-English help; Automatic Spell Checking marks misspellings as you type.

Templates

One of Word's most powerful features has always been its use of document templates. The new version of Word makes your life even easier by providing an expanded collection of pre-written templates (see Figure A.4) that you can use. The use of templates is covered in Lesson 4. You may want to browse through Word's new template offerings to see what's available. Note: The templates that are available to you will depend on options selected when Word is installed on your system.

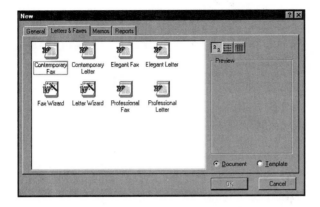

FIGURE A.4   Word for Windows 95 provides an expanded collection of prewritten templates.

E-MAIL

If your computer is hooked up to a Microsoft-compatible electronic mail system, you'll find Word's new E-mail capabilities to be a great time saver. E-mail is not covered in this book. Please refer to your Word documentation on on-line Help for more information.

WINDOWS 95 PRIMER

Microsoft Windows 95 is a graphical operating system that makes your computer easy to use by providing menus and pictures to select. Before you can take advantage of it, however, you must learn some Windows 95 basics.

A FIRST LOOK AT WINDOWS 95

You don't have to start Windows 95—it starts automatically when you turn on your PC. After the initial startup screens, you arrive at a screen something like the one shown in Figure B.1. (Notice how the open programs look on the Taskbar in Figure B.1.)

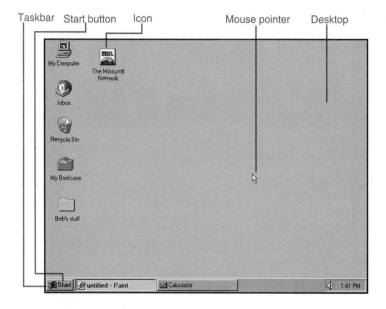

FIGURE B.1 The Windows 95 screen.

PARTS OF THE SCREEN

As shown in Figure B.1, the Windows 95 screen contains many special elements and controls. Here's a brief summary:

- The background on which all the pictures and boxes rest is the *desktop*.

- The *Taskbar* shows the windows and programs that are open. You can switch between open windows and programs by clicking the name on the Taskbar.

- The *Start button* opens a menu system from which you can start programs. Click on the Start button; then, click on your selection from each menu that appears.

- Some *icons* appear on your desktop—you can activate one by double-clicking on it.

You'll learn more about these elements as we continue.

 Also Appearing... If your computer has Microsoft Office installed on it, you see the Office Shortcuts toolbar on-screen too. It's a series of little pictures strung together horizontally, representing Office programs. Hold the mouse over a picture to see what it does; click on it to launch the program. See your Microsoft Office documentation to learn more.

USING A MOUSE

To work most efficiently in Windows, you need a mouse. Here are the mouse actions you need to know:

- *Point* means to move the mouse pointer onto the specified item by moving the mouse. The tip of the mouse pointer must touch the item.

- *Click* on an item means to move the pointer onto the specified item and press and release the mouse button once. Unless specified otherwise (i.e. right-click), use the left mouse button. Clicking usually selects an item.

- *Double-click* on an item means to move the pointer to the specified item and press and release the left mouse button twice quickly. Double-clicking usually activates an item.

- *Drag* means to move the mouse pointer onto the item, hold down the mouse button, and move the mouse while holding down the button. Unless specified (i.e. right-drag), use the left mouse button.

CONTROLLING A WINDOW WITH THE MOUSE

Windows are the heart of the Windows 95 program. Windows 95 sections off these rectangular areas for particular purposes, such as running a program. You can control a window using the procedures shown in Figure B.2.

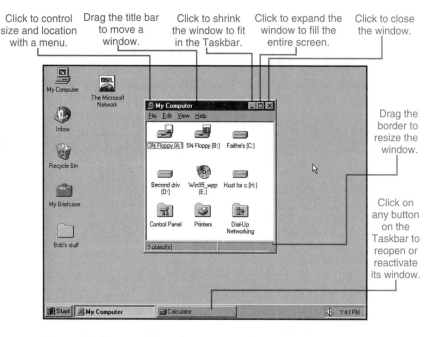

FIGURE **B.2**   Use your mouse to control windows.

Scroll Bars If your window contains more icons than it can display at once, scroll bars appear on the bottom and/or right edges of the window. To move through the window's contents, click on an arrow button at either end of a scroll bar to move in that direction, or drag the gray bar in the direction you want to move.

GETTING HELP

Windows 95 comes with a great on-line Help system. To access it, click your mouse on the Start button, and click on Help. You see the box shown in Figure B.3.

FIGURE B.3 Windows offers several kinds of help.

There are three tabs in this box: Contents, Index, and Find. The Contents tab appears on top first. To move to a tab, click on it. Here's how to use each tab:

- Contents Double-click on any book to open it. Sub-books and documents appear. Double-click on sub-books and documents to open them.

- Index   Type the word you want to look up. The Index list scrolls to that part of the alphabetical listing. When you see the topic on the list that you want to read, double-click on it.

- Find   The first time you click on this tab, Windows tells you it needs to create a list. Click Next, and Finish to allow this. Then you see the main Find tab. Type the word you want to find in the top text box. Then click a word in the middle box to narrow the search. Finally, review the list of help topics at the bottom, and double-click the one you want to read.

When you're done reading about a document, click Help Topics to return to the main Help screen, or click Back to return to the previous Help topic. Or, click the window's Close button to exit Help.

Starting a Program

There are many ways to start a program, but here is the simplest (see Figure B.4):

1. Click the Start button.

2. Click Programs.

3. Click on the group that contains the program you want to start (for instance, Microsoft Office 95).

4. Click on the program you want to start (for instance, Microsoft Access).

Another way to start a program is to open a document that you created in that program—the program automatically opens when the document opens. Double-click on a document file in My Computer or Windows Explorer to open it, or click the Start button and select a recently-used document from the Documents menu.

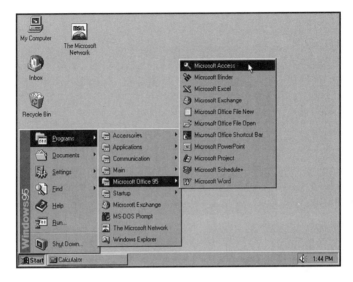

FIGURE B.4   Click on the Start button; then, click on each menu and submenu, until you find the program you want to start.

You can also start a program by double-clicking on its shortcut icon on the desktop. Shortcut icons are links to other files. When you use a shortcut, Windows simply follows the link back to the original file.

Whenever you use a document or program frequently, you might consider creating a shortcut for it on the desktop. To do so, just use the right mouse button to drag an object out of Windows Explorer or My Computer. On the shortcut menu that appears, select Create Shortcut(s) Here.

Using Menus

Almost all Windows programs have menu bars containing menus. The menu names appear across the top of the screen in a row. To open a menu, click on its name. The menu drops down, displaying its commands. To select a command, click on it.

Shortcut Keys Notice in Figure B.5 that key names, such as Enter for the Open command or F8 for the Copy command, appear after some command names. These are shortcut keys. You use these keys to perform the commands without opening the menu.

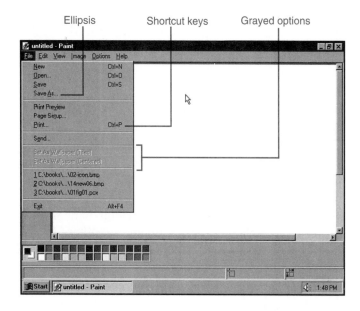

FIGURE B.5 A menu lists various commands you can perform.

Usually, when you select a command, Windows 95 executes the command immediately. However:

- If the command name is gray (instead of black), the command is unavailable at the moment and you cannot choose it.

- If the command name is followed by an arrow, as with the Start button's menus, selecting the command causes another menu to appear, from which you must make another selection.

- If the command is followed by an ellipsis (three dots), selecting it will cause a dialog box to appear. You'll learn about dialog boxes in the next section.

USING SHORTCUT MENUS

A new feature in Windows 95 is the shortcut menu. Right-click on any object (any icon, screen element, file or folder, etc.), and a shortcut menu appears, as shown in Figure B.6. The shortcut menu contains commands that apply only to the selected object. Click on any command to select it, or click outside the menu to cancel.

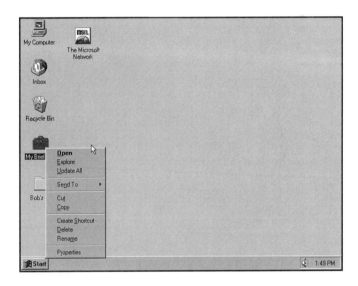

FIGURE B.6   Shortcut menus are new for Windows 95.

NAVIGATING DIALOG BOXES

A dialog box is the operating system's way of requesting additional information. For example, if you choose Print from the File menu of the WordPad application, you see a dialog box something like the one shown in Figure B.7. (Its exact look will vary depending on your printer.)

Option button   Tab   Drop-down list

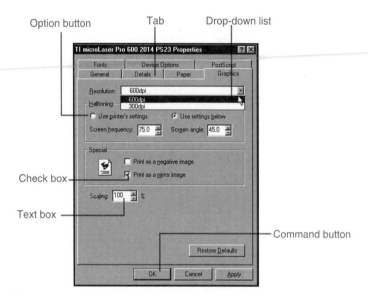

FIGURE B.7   A dialog box requests additional information.

Each dialog box contains one or more of the following elements:

- *Tabs* bring up additional "pages" of options you can choose. Click on a tab to activate it.

- *List boxes* display available choices. Click on any item on the list to select it. If the entire list is not visible, use the scroll bar to find additional choices.

- *Drop-down lists* are similar to list boxes, but only one item in the list is shown. To see the rest of the list, click the down arrow to the right of the list box. Then click on an item to select it.

- *Text boxes* enable you to type in an entry. Just click inside the text box and type. Text boxes that expect numeric input usually have up and down arrow buttons (increment buttons) that let you bump the number up and down.

- *Check boxes* enable you to turn on or off an individual option. Click on a check box to turn it on or off. Each check box is an independent unit that doesn't affect other check boxes.

- *Option buttons* are like check boxes, but option buttons appear in groups, and you can select only one. When you select an option button, PowerPoint deselects any others you already selected. Click on a button to activate it.

- *Command buttons* perform an action, such as executing the options you set, closing the dialog box, or opening another dialog box. To select a command button, click on it.

FROM HERE...

If you need more help with Windows 95, I suggest one of these books:

The Complete Idiot's Guide to Windows 95 by Paul McFedries

Windows 95 Cheat Sheet by Joe Kraynak

The Big Basics Book of Windows 95 by Shelley O'Hara, Jennifer Fulton, and Ed Guilford

INDEX

T

PLUG YOURSELF INTO...

THE MACMILLAN INFORMATION SUPERLIBRARY™

Free information and vast computer resources from the world's leading computer book publisher—online!

FIND THE BOOKS THAT ARE RIGHT FOR YOU!
A complete online catalog, plus sample chapters and tables of contents!

- ● STAY INFORMED with the latest computer industry news through our online newsletter, press releases, and customized Information SuperLibrary Reports.
- ● GET FAST ANSWERS to your questions about MCP books.
- ● VISIT our online bookstore for the latest information and editions!
- ● COMMUNICATE with our expert authors through e-mail and conferences.
- ● DOWNLOAD SOFTWARE from the immense MCP library:
  - Source code, shareware, freeware, and demos
- ● DISCOVER HOT SPOTS on other parts of the Internet.
- ● WIN BOOKS in ongoing contests and giveaways!

TO PLUG INTO MCP:

WORLD WIDE WEB: **http://www.mcp.com**

GOPHER: gopher.mcp.com   FTP: ftp.mcp.com

Complete and Return this Card
for a *FREE* Computer Book Catalog

Thank you for purchasing this book! You have purchased a superior computer book written expressly for your needs. To continue to provide the kind of up-to-date, pertinent coverage you've come to expect from us, we need to hear from you. Please take a minute to complete and return this self-addressed, postage-paid form. In return, we'll send you a free catalog of all our computer books on topics ranging from word processing to programming and the internet.

Mr. ☐   Mrs. ☐   Ms. ☐   Dr. ☐

Name (first) ☐☐☐☐☐☐☐☐☐☐☐ (M.I.) ☐ (last) ☐☐☐☐☐☐☐☐☐☐☐☐☐☐☐

Address ☐☐☐☐☐☐☐☐☐☐☐☐☐☐☐☐☐☐☐☐☐☐☐☐☐☐☐

☐☐☐☐☐☐☐☐☐☐☐☐☐☐☐☐☐☐☐☐☐☐☐☐☐☐☐

City ☐☐☐☐☐☐☐☐☐☐☐☐☐ State ☐☐ Zip ☐☐☐☐☐ ☐☐☐☐

Phone ☐☐☐ ☐☐☐ ☐☐☐☐ Fax ☐☐☐ ☐☐☐ ☐☐☐☐

Company Name ☐☐☐☐☐☐☐☐☐☐☐☐☐☐☐☐☐☐☐☐☐

E-mail address ☐☐☐☐☐☐☐☐☐☐☐☐☐☐☐☐☐☐☐☐☐☐☐☐☐☐

1. Please check at least (3) influencing factors for purchasing this book.

Front or back cover information on book .... ☐
Special approach to the content .... ☐
Completeness of content .... ☐
Author's reputation .... ☐
Publisher's reputation .... ☐
Book cover design or layout .... ☐
Index or table of contents of book .... ☐
Price of book .... ☐
Special effects, graphics, illustrations .... ☐
Other (Please specify): _____ ☐

2. How did you first learn about this book?

Internet Site .... ☐
Saw in Macmillan Computer
  Publishing catalog .... ☐
Recommended by store personnel .... ☐
Saw the book on bookshelf at store .... ☐
Recommended by a friend .... ☐
Received advertisement in the mail .... ☐
Saw an advertisement in: _____ ☐
Read book review in: _____ ☐
Other (Please specify): _____ ☐

3. How many computer books have you purchased in the last six months?

This book only .... ☐   3 to 5 books .... ☐
2 books .... ☐   More than 5 .... ☐

4. Where did you purchase this book?

Bookstore .... ☐
Computer Store .... ☐
Consumer Electronics Store .... ☐
Department Store .... ☐
Office Club .... ☐
Warehouse Club .... ☐
Mail Order .... ☐
Direct from Publisher .... ☐
Internet site .... ☐
Other (Please specify): .... ☐

5. How long have you been using a computer?

Less than 6 months .. ☐   6 months to a year ..... ☐
1 to 3 years .... ☐   More than 3 years ...... ☐

6. What is your level of experience with personal computers and with the subject of this book?

	With PC's	With subject of book
New	☐	☐
Casual	☐	☐
Accomplished	☐	☐
Expert	☐	☐

Source Code — ISBN: 0-7897-0379-3

7. Which of the following best describes your job title?

Administrative Assistant ☐
Coordinator ☐
Manager/Supervisor ☐
Director ☐
Vice President ☐
President/CEO/COO ☐
Lawyer/Doctor/Medical Professional ☐
Teacher/Educator/Trainer ☐
Engineer/Technician ☐
Consultant ☐
Not employed/Student/Retired ☐
Other (Please specify): ☐

8. Which of the following best describes the area of the company your job title falls under?

Accounting ☐
Engineering ☐
Manufacturing ☐
Marketing ☐
Operations ☐
Sales ☐
Other (Please specify): ☐

9. What is your age?

Under 20 ☐
21-29 ☐
30-39 ☐
40-49 ☐
50-59 ☐
60-over ☐

10. Are you:

Male ☐
Female ☐

11. Which computer publications do you read regularly? (Please list)

_____
_____
_____
_____
_____
_____
_____
_____
_____

Comments: _____
_____
_____

Fold here and scotch-tape to m

llı'ı'ı'ı'ı'ı''ıll'ı'ı'ı'ı''ıll'ı''ıll'ı'ıl